Nirvana

The Cranberries

KRS One

Soundgarden

Soundgarden

Joey Ramone

SLACKER

SLACKER

1991, TEEN SPIRIT ANGST, AND THE GENERATION IT CREATED

ROB JANICKE

FOUNDER OF GENERATION RIFF

SLACKER by Rob Janicke

Copyright © 2024 Rob Janicke

Published by Inspired By You Books, an imprint of Inspired Girl Publishing Group, a division of Inspired Girl Enterprises
Asbury Park, NJ 07712
www.inspiredgirlenterprises.com

Inspired Girl is honored to bring forth books with heart that connect us to our personal power and to one another. We are proud to offer this book to our readers; the stories, the experiences, the advice, and the words are the author's alone.

The events are portrayed to the best of the author's memory. The author has tried to recreate events, locales, and conversations from his memories of them. The conversations in the book all come from the author's recollections, though they are not written to represent word-for-word transcripts. Rather, the author has retold them in a way that evokes the feeling and meaning of what was said. In all instances, the essence of the dialogue is accurate.

This book is written as a source of information only. Although the author and publisher have made every effort to ensure that the information in this book was correct at press time, the author and publisher do not assume and hereby disclaim any liability to any party for any loss, damage, or disruption caused by errors or omissions, whether such errors or omissions result from negligence, accident, or any other cause. Adherence to all applicable laws and regulations, including international, federal, state and local governing professional licensing, business practices, advertising, and all other aspects of doing business in the US, Canada or any other jurisdiction is the sole responsibility of the reader and consumer. Neither the author nor the publisher assumes any responsibility or liability whatsoever on behalf of the consumer or reader of this material. Any perceived slight of any individual or organization is purely unintentional.

The author and publisher do not assume and hereby disclaim any liability in connection with the use of the information contained in this book. Products, pictures, trademarks, and trademark names are used throughout this book to describe and inform the reader about various proprietary products that are owned by third parties. No endorsement of the information contained in this book is given by the owners of such products and trademarks, and no endorsement is implied by the inclusion of products, pictures, or trademarks in this book.

© 2024 Rob Janicke

All rights reserved. No portion of this book may be reproduced in any form without permission from the publisher, except as permitted by U.S. copyright law. For permissions contact: help@inspiredgirlenterprises.com

ISBN: 978-1-965240-12-0

Creative & Editorial Director: Jenn Tuma-Young
Book Packaging and Design: Inspired Girl Publishing Group
Book Cover Design: Andrej Semnic
Typeset: Roseanna White Designs
Copy Editor: Janelle Leonard
Author Photo (back cover): Bridget Helene Photography
Photo Credit (pages 1 and 4): Jared Miller

Printed in the USA

DEDICATION

For my wife Amy, daughter Peyton, son Michael, and canine baby, Rocky

This book is also for my fellow SLACKERS worldwide who feel music more than they hear it, are energized by and inspired to do great things with it and share their love and excitement for it at every turn.

CONTENTS

FOREWORD: ABOUT A MIXTAPE
13

PLAYLIST
19

CHAPTER 1 – THE CONNECTION
Feeling Music and Its Lasting Effects
21

CHAPTER 2 – 1984: THE INFLUENCE BEGINS
Beneath the Façade of Bubble Gum, the Roots of Grunge Grow
33

CHAPTER 3 – 1985: CONCERTS AND FUNDRAISERS
The Power of People Coming Together Through Music
49

CHAPTER 4 – 1986: THE MUSIC WORLD IS BREAKING UP
Genre-bending Is Breaking the Ground for Grunge
61

CHAPTER 5 – 1987: GRUNGE SPROUT ROOTS
When the Term Grunge Started Its Journey Toward Commercialization
73

CHAPTER 6 – 1988-1990: IT'S ALWAYS DARKEST BEFORE THE DAWN
A Society in Turmoil and the Music to Follow
85

CHAPTER 7 – 1991: THE EXPLOSION
We Have Liftoff
99

CHAPTER 8 – 1992-1993: THIS IS DANGEROUS
The Angst Got Angstier
129

CHAPTER 9 – 1994: THE SHOT HEARD AROUND THE WORLD
Crash of the King and the Pending Doom
159

CHAPTER 10 – 1995-1996: CAPITALIZING ON IT ALL
The Advertising World Was Not Ready for It to Be Over
171

CHAPTER 11 – 1997-1998: THE TIMES, THEY ARE A-CHANGIN'
We Are Conflicted
195

CHAPTER 12 – 1999: BUBBLEGUM IS BACK
Pop Music and Technology Left Grunge with Nothing but Cavities
209

CHAPTER 13 – FROM A SLACKER
More of a Confession Than a Chapter
223

ACKNOWLEDGMENTS
225

FOREWORD
ABOUT A MIXTAPE

"I FOUND IT HARD, IT'S HARD TO FIND. OH WELL, WHATEVER, NEVER MIND."

These lyrics making up the final verse of the Nirvana song that blew up the world in 1991, "Smells Like Teen Spirit," (off the bands' sophomore album *Nevermind*) could be the rallying cry and epitaph of every GenX kid from 1991 through today. Described as disaffected youth and depressed slackers who would amount to nothing, these words were as timely and fitting as could be. Looking back, they still are.

Significant historical moments are usually discussed in the "where were you when" type of conversation. My parents, and their entire generation, would always discuss the JFK assassination that way. Older cousins of mine or brothers and sisters of my friends had their version of that when referencing the murder of John Lennon in 1980. I was only seven years old at the time and vaguely remember the news coverage, but I couldn't tell you where I was the first time I'd heard about the shooting. I remember the first time I'd ever heard music by Nirvana. Oh, the days of mixtapes, how I miss them.

I was given one mixtape that has had an indelible impact on me, way back in 1989. I was given this cassette by a high school friend named Pat. Pat was that friend we all tend to have—you know, the one who seems to know all the cool music before anyone else does. Of course, he liked and knew The Beatles and the Stones, but he took you so much further. Along with those massive radio bands, Pat knew and liked other bands as well. Bands people like me didn't know existed. The MC5, Iggy and the Stooges, dozens of '60s garage and psychedelic bands. When he handed me the tape, I was intrigued and I knew my life would never be the same again.

This piece of plastic, with Pat's handwriting on the inner sleeve, changed me forever. This cassette given to me in 1989, this prophetic gift of music, introduced me to what, just a few short years later, (1991 to be exact) the rest of the world would lose their collective shit over.

The music collected on the tape was a *"who's who"* of who would become some of the biggest names in a new genre, alternative and/or grunge music. Bands such as Nirvana, Soundgarden, Violent Femmes, Jane's Addiction, Red Hot Chili Peppers, Sonic Youth, Mudhoney, Fugazi, and more. I know I'm probably forgetting some of the bands, but as you can see, this was a launching pad for me. This was the high diving board at the pool. Once you jumped, you couldn't possibly go back.

With headphones firmly in place, I started listening to the mixtape over and over again. It propelled me to a new sound. Although I didn't know it at the time, that sound would signify a lifelong obsession with the music contained in it. I heard the sounds and felt the words I knew were about to change my life forever. I may have only been a teenager in high school, but there was a seismic shift in how this music was hitting me. One song in particular was a mid-tempo, jangly-guitar track that felt different to me than songs I'd heard before. It was dark yet melodic, it was desperate yet hopeful. The singer's voice was different but instantaneously comforting. The song was "About a Girl", the band was Nirvana, and the singer was Kurt Cobain. It was off their debut album, *Bleach*. It wasn't heavy, it wasn't loud, but it was different from the other music that was out at that time. It begins with a swaying,

FOREWORD: ABOUT A MIXTAPE

jangly guitar intro (something that would become a bit of a signature sound for the band in years to come) and it sucked me in. It had a familiar quality to it though, it was melodic and catchy, almost like a Beatles song. Of course, now we all know what a huge influence The Beatles were to Kurt Cobain, and describing one of their songs as having hints of The Beatles in it is common. Back in 1989 though, I didn't even know the names of the band members, let alone who their favorite musicians were. So, I gravitated to this song and called Pat to learn more about it and the band who wrote it. He told me the song title, the band, and the album. With the information I'd just learned, I asked another friend of mine, Frank, if he wanted to go to Sam Goody (a large music store chain) with me to look for a CD I wanted to buy. He was down and asked the name of the band I was talking about. Frank was a movie guy, and he knew I was a music guy. Neither one of us always knew what the other one was talking about, especially when it was something new and not popular. So, when I told him it was a band called Nirvana, and I was looking for an album called *Bleach*, he paused and said, "What are they called, Nevada?" with a look on his face that told me I was crazy. He wasn't wrong though because almost NO ONE, outside of Seattle, had heard of Nirvana yet. If I hadn't been given the tape by Pat, I'd probably think the band was called Nevada as well. Looking back though, it's almost impossible to remember a time in which Nirvana wasn't in the global consciousness.

    I feel music in a very deep way. I breathe it in, it gets stored in my soul and in my blood. I need it to live. I'd like to think I was on my way to that before the infamous tape, but I'll never truly know. What I do know is this, that tape, my friendship with Pat at the time, our conversations, and the musical education I received from him, are as responsible for my love of music as anything else. Thank you, Pat!!

    When I first decided to write this book, it began with a simple enough concept. Music can shape, change, and guide generations. It can promote social change and progressive thought and give meaning to individual lives that may have been lost otherwise. It's one of the most powerful forces we have as human beings. This was true for the 1960s and the world changed for good after its work was done.

Interestingly, this book is about thirty+ years of discussions surrounding the effects of a global musical revolution beginning in 1991, thirty years after the movement of the '60s. I believe music has always been cyclical. It's always seemed to have some very effective years but inevitably becomes stale. A new voice is always needed, and one is always lurking. In this case, the messages conveyed by the progress of the '60s had all but died come the 1980s. Music is somehow good at recognizing when this happens. Kids pick up guitars, get behind drum kits, and start writing words and thoughts that come from a place in their souls they can no longer ignore. That's when it happens. That's when the previous musical revolution takes its final breath as an arbiter of change and dies. It's an energy people tend to feel and take heed of its importance. Once the spark is lit, the fire ignites, and we just wait for the explosion.

Although it doesn't feel like more than thirty years have passed since that glorious explosion of 1991, they have. The years have come and gone in what feels like the blink of an eye, or better yet, in a loud and sweaty instant of a crowd-surfing escapade from the middle of a packed club in New York City to the stage of a band playing its heart out. It goes by quickly but it's one of the best rides you'll ever take. I was eighteen in 1991, and I was primed for a revolution, and it happened. Now, thirty years later, I'm a married father of two young children and a music writer. Life has so many expected and unexpected twists and turns to it, but one thing remains constant, the music. I knew something was happening back then; the music scene was palpable. It had a heartbeat, a pulse. It breathed fire and it blasted through the atmosphere like a rocket ship not caring where it was going or if it would even reach its destination safely. It changed my life. It changed the world.

I was there, along with millions of others, not as a musician, but as a fan, a member of the scene, and someone who's chronicled its history all along the

FOREWORD: ABOUT A MIXTAPE

way. I was in the room when Grunge was born, I was there when it died. I am Gen X. I am Generation Riff. I am *SLACKER*!

Now I might not have made you a mixtape, but I did make you a Spotify playlist. You'll find the QR code to the playlist on the next page. Listen to it as you read through my story, the history, along with interviews and quotes from those who were on the frontlines of the grunge revolution as well as commentary from sociologists and psychologists as you dig into 1991, teen spirit angst, and the generation it created!

PLAYLIST

CREATED BY CARD-CARRYING MEMBER OF GENERATION X, MUSIC HISTORIAN, GRUNGE AFICIONADO... AUTHOR OF *SLACKER*, ROB JANICKE

..........................FEATURING SONGS FROM..........................

NIRVANA / PEARL JAM / STONE TEMPLE PILOTS / GREEN DAY / BUSH
ALICE IN CHAINS / SMASHING PUMPKINS / SOUND GARDEN
TEMPLE OF THE DOG / ALANIS MORISSETTE / THE CRANBERRIES
JEWEL / R.E.M. / COLLECTIVE SOUL / RADIOHEAD / LIVE
SOUL ASYLUM / BLIND MELON / FOO FIGHTERS / AND MORE...

CHAPTER 1
THE CONNECTION: FEELING MUSIC AND ITS LASTING EFFECTS

"IS IT POSITIVE?" I NERVOUSLY ASKED MY WIFE AMY, WONDERING IF SHE WAS ABOUT TO deliver the news that would change the course of the rest of our lives. Was "Dad" about to replace my given name and identity? Amy didn't say a word as she handed me the small, plastic device that somehow held the information that would tell us whether we were expecting our first child.

I slowly extended my hand, almost not wanting to take hold of this drugstore-bought crystal ball because I knew that once it was in my possession I would be obligated to look down at my future.

"Is that a plus symbol? It looks like a plus symbol to me. Plus means positive, right? So, you're pregnant? Are we positive? Because this thing seems pretty positive."

Ok, I probably didn't need to ask so many questions but when you're in that moment for the first time you have no idea what it feels like until it's happening. In my case, as a thirty-nine-year-old man who is the product of divorce and had proclaimed for as long as I could remember that I was never getting married or having kids, you can start to understand my rapid-fire questioning tactics. I had already reneged on one of the promises I made to myself by getting married, and now I was about to go 2 for 2 in the defiance department regarding my lifelong proclamations.

Don't get me wrong, I was thrilled that we were about to become parents and that I was going to be a dad. It was an excitement I'd never felt before. Soon after the waves of elation broke over me, the fear set in. Hold up, am I about to become responsible for the life of another human being? I'm going to have to raise a child in a world I'm as unsure about today as on the day I was born. When we face new challenges, we sometimes look to our past as a guide, a beacon of light to pave the way. The problem with that way of thinking is that it assumes you have a healthy past to pull from. The issue for me was that my parents got divorced, and my dad moved out when I was just five years old. My sister was only three. I didn't know it at the time, but this event was going to shape my life in ways I'd come to hate from that moment on.

It took a while, four years to be exact, for the first hammer to fall on me from the divorce. I was always an open and honest kid when it came to describing how I felt in a particular situation. Be it positive or negative, I expressed what my inner voice was telling me. At nine years old, I told my mom that I no longer wanted to live. Nine years old. That's heavy. As I write this, my children are ten and eight respectively and if either of them told me they didn't want to live anymore, to say I'd panic would be the understatement of the century. To my mother's credit, she didn't panic, at least not outwardly, and instead enrolled me in therapy. I can remember the room with the bookshelves on the left of the table I'd sit at, which was across from the play area I'd punch stuffed animals in to express my anger toward my parents not being together and my dad not living with us anymore. I'll never forget those days.

As those shapes I mentioned above turned into anger, isolation, insecurity, depression, and suicidal thoughts that had been somewhat silent companions of mine for decades, the events and memories associated with them throughout my life, rose to the surface. A surface I could barely tread at times. I knew nothing about being a husband and here I was, less than a year into

CHAPTER 1: THE CONNECTION: FEELING MUSIC AND ITS LASTING EFFECTS

my marriage. The same lack of knowledge applied to my ability to become a father. In a word, I was petrified.

With all my new concerns and past mindsets about the world and my place in it, I was beyond worried about the damage I could do to this precious new life that would soon grace the lives of Amy and me. Would my lifelong battle with depression slither its destructive way into my baby and infect him or her with the heaviness and overwhelming debris attached to it? What would happen if the two occasions when I thought it would be better to leave the planet than stick around and figure it all out found their way to my child's thoughts and did the same thing to that innocent soul? How could I justify this decision Amy and I made to have a baby when I still had so many demons and unanswered questions?

I was interviewing Nico Hoon, the daughter of Blind Melon's singer/songwriter, Shannon Hoon, for this book when we stumbled upon an eerie, yet proof-positive connection that explains why alternative music from the 1990s means so much to so many. Our conversation could be viewed as a microcosm of this entire book. I wrote *SLACKER*, in part, to discuss and even marvel at the fact that what happened musically and culturally in the late 1980s/early '90s was due to honesty and vulnerability in popular music we hadn't witnessed before. The effects were so massive and personal to those listening, that they helped create the people they'd become for generations. Probably the entirety of their lives.

Formed in 1990, Blind Melon became a multi-platinum-selling band just three short years later, largely due to the success of their video (directed by Samuel Bayer) for the single "No Rain" off the band's self-titled, debut album which was released in 1992. As the band grew in popularity, frontman Shannon Hoon shot to celebrity status, as a prolific songwriter and respected musician. Some people are quick to lump Blind Melon into the one-hit wonder bin of '90s rock because of the enormous appeal and reach of "No Rain." Those in the know, however, understand that this was not the case. Granted, the band never did achieve the commercial success of their infamous single, but the songs on both their debut, as well as their follow-up, *Soup* (1995), rank amongst some of the best of the era.

One track in particular was the focus of my interview with Nico.

Nico Blue Hoon, born just months before her father's death on October 21, 1995, was twenty-eight-years-old at the time of our interview in 2022, the same age as Shannon when he passed away. The song is called "New Life," the 12th track on the band's sophomore album, *Soup*. If you read the lyrics, one cannot mistake what Shannon was writing about. If you listen to the song though, you will *feel* the honesty, vulnerability, and sheer desperation in Hoon's voice. The song was written from Shannon's perspective upon receiving the news that he was going to become a father. It was no secret that Shannon had demons and struggled with substance abuse at different times throughout his life. His lyrics reflected this, along with countless interviews he granted over the course of his career, and "New Life" was the ultimate tribute to the idea that he needed to clean up.

During my conversation with Nico, I told her what a huge impact this song had on me. It was quite surreal for me to be telling the young woman who the song was written about before she was even born, and who tragically lost her dad to addiction, that Shannon's words had pushed me to change in ways I knew I needed to be a great dad to my daughter.

After finally realizing that the symbol on my wife's pregnancy test was a plus sign and that she was indeed pregnant, pending a doctor's visit of course, Blind Melon's "New Life" instantly started playing in my head. It was an event that would force me to become more aware and present than ever before. Remember, *Soup*, which contains "New Life" was released in 1995, and my wife and I found out about our child (who we would learn was a girl a few months later) in 2012. My math skills do not rank up there with generational mathematicians such as Euclid or even fictional ones like Will Hunting, but I do know that those dates are seventeen years apart. How, during what was the

CHAPTER 1: THE CONNECTION: FEELING MUSIC AND ITS LASTING EFFECTS

most incredible moment of my life up until that point, does my brain rewind itself to think of a song released seventeen years earlier?

Speaking with Dr. Kelly Jakubowski, an Assistant Professor in Music Psychology at Durham University, in Durham, England, music and memory have multiple links.

"We attach more salience to memories from a certain time period in our lives. We have a lot of really important and self-defining memories during that time when we defined who we are. Comparing music against other types of memory cues, what we've found quite consistently across several studies now, is that music seems to be somewhat unique in doing this." Dr. Jakubowski has researched and written on topics including memory for music, music-evoked autobiographical memory, musical imagery and imagination, and cross-cultural music perception, among other music and memory-related topics. Her work has been published in *The New York Times, The Guardian, The Wall Street Journal, Psychology Today*, and many other print and digital news outlets. I now understand how I was jettisoned back seventeen years at a moment's notice and why it was music that provided the journey.

So, for the next nine months, without many days off, I listened to "New Life" at least once a day to remind myself that I needed to make sure I was ok and would be capable of giving my daughter the happy, confident, and loving father she so deserved. If you're a parent, you quickly come to realize that no one has a rule book to hand you. You leave the hospital with the clothes on your back, a human being that is less than a week old, and a mind full of questions and fears you have exactly zero answers for. I guess you can pull from your experience as a child and how you were raised by your parents but that's iffy at best. What if you didn't have the best childhood? Some kids, like me, were raised by a single parent so an upbringing such as that can skew things in a certain direction.

Divorce was relatively uncommon before 1970 but that would drastically change. According to research by W. Bradford Wilcox in "The Evolution of Divorce" for National Affairs, from 1960 to 1980, the divorce rate more than doubled—from 9.2 divorces per 1,000 married women to 22.6 divorces per 1,000 married women. This meant that while less than 20% of couples who married in 1950 ended up divorced, about 50% of couples who married in 1970 did. Approximately half of the children born to married parents in the 1970s saw their parent's part, compared to only about 11% of those born in the 1950s.

Studies show divorce has a multitude of negative effects on children and some of them are outlined in *Growing Up with a Single Parent: What Helps, What Hurts* by sociologists Sara McLanahan and Gary Sandefur. According to their research, since 1974, about 1 million children have seen their parents' divorce each year. Those children are two to three times more likely than their peers from intact marriages to suffer from serious social or psychological pathologies. The authors found that 31% of adolescents from divorced parents dropped out of high school compared to 13% of children from intact families. They also concluded that 33% of adolescent girls whose parents divorced became teen mothers compared to 11% of girls from continuously married families. In addition, the sociologists found that 11% of boys who come from divorced families end up spending time in prison before the age of 32, compared to 5% of boys who come from intact homes.

Perhaps one of the most sobering statistics comes from sociologist Paul Amato who estimates that if the United States enjoyed the same amount of marital stability today as we did in 1960, we'd have roughly 600,000 fewer children in therapy and approximately 70,000 fewer suicide attempts each year.

Life is strange though, because just when you feel as lost and scared as you've ever been, something as seemingly simple as a song can save your life. It sounds impossible, but it's not. In my case, a song written by a man I'd never met, nearly two decades before my child was born, somehow gave me

CHAPTER 1: THE CONNECTION: FEELING MUSIC AND ITS LASTING EFFECTS

the confidence I'd need to believe I'd be ok. My child would be ok. Life would be ok. I will not pretend to understand how all this works, I just know that for me, it did.

When I told Nico this story, she reminisced about her reaction to the track.

"That one is a tearjerker, and it also shows how strong my mom is," Nico said. She continued, "It's weird to hear a song about you being born before you were born. It means a lot to me, and I know it means a lot to my mom because when you have a loved one pass away it is super hard, and that song is something for her to look back on and how she shared that special connection with my dad."

Nico and I talked about other topics aside from "New Life" and the bond we share because of it. We discussed what it's like for her to have a dad that she doesn't remember yet was a hero to legions of fans around the world. The power of Blind Melon's music has connected her to her dad, through the love of his songs, and by the band's large and loyal fanbase.

Nico said, "It's very cool to know that people are still thinking about his music all these years later," as we continued our discussion about his, and Blind Melon's influence on the '90s music scene and beyond.

Aside from the global success of the band's most popular song, "No Rain," Hoon's vocals and lyrics would become a major part of their legacy which can be heard and felt to this day. The vulnerability of the messages in many of Blind Melon's songs and the raw, uncompromising lyrics Hoon would sing were almost a genre unto themselves. Southern bands such as Kings of Leon, The Black Keys, Cage the Elephant, and The Avett Brothers have all made use of blues-influenced Southern rock and integrated the stripped-down element we've heard in modern and alternative rock in the decades following Hoon's death.

While discussing The Avett Brothers' love of songs that juxtapose a cheery melody with harsh and honest lyrical introspection in *American Song-*

writer Magazine (2009), Seth Avett had this to say about Blind Melon's lasting influence, "You'll find that a fair amount in Blind Melon's music (the juxtaposition between cheery melodies and harsh, honest lyrics). Shannon Hoon had the most beautiful and joyous voice while he was talking about the most heart-wrenching challenges, self-doubt, pain, and confusion. He made it sound so sweet. What an apt description of people in general. We're all complicated, and we all have a way of being two ways at once."

As you will come to find out as you continue through the book, I'm a big Pearl Jam fan. I've seen them live over thirty times, with my first time coming at Lollapalooza II, in 1992. I mention this here because Nico also told me that Shannon was a huge Pearl Jam fan as well, and Nico got to see them for the first time when they played the Sea Hear Now festival in Asbury Park, New Jersey in 2021. When this came up in our interview, Nico said, "I feel like I gravitate more toward indie music than straight-up rock. Plus, I'm a really big folk-rock fan. But then I saw Pearl Jam and they opened my eyes because I had never really listened to their music before. There was this interview with my dad that was kind of cool where he was talking about his view of Pearl Jam so now it's cool to say that I've seen them in concert too. I got to see and understand what he was talking about in that interview. And the best part is, I saw them before I ever saw the interview with my dad, so it was cool to develop my own feelings for them."

I asked Nico if her feelings lined up similarly with her dad's. "They're not the band I'll always put on, but I found my own love for them, and I really enjoy listening to them because I knew they really meant a lot to my dad and that's a cool connection I can have with him. When I hear them now, it's emotional for me because he was such a huge fan of that band and then I start thinking about everything. And when I saw them at Sea Hear Now, it was so emotional because I kept thinking that I wish my dad could be here to watch this with me."

Long before the idea for this book was conceived, I had an experience

CHAPTER 1: THE CONNECTION: FEELING MUSIC AND ITS LASTING EFFECTS

that proved to me that my ability to *feel* music, and the importance the art form has in my life, was more than just notes played on instruments. This is about human connection.

In 2005, I injured my neck/spine and had to have surgery. I was thirty-two years old, in decent shape, and pulled through with flying colors. This was important because I knew rehab and physical therapy were looming and assumed I'd get through the rehab with ease. I had things to do, places to go, and people to see. Sitting alone in my room, missing out on life wasn't part of the plan. Tops on my list of things to do, places to go, and people to see, were centered around my love of music and nothing was going to stop me. Until it did.

Mike McCready, Peal Jam's lead guitarist, had an event scheduled in Seattle right around the time I was beginning my post-surgery rehab. McCready was diagnosed with Crohn's disease, a debilitating inflammatory bowel disease, causing inflammation in your digestive tract, which currently does not have a cure. He has been a long-time, national spokesperson for the Crohn's & Colitis Foundation throughout his career with Pearl Jam. McCready was hosting a fundraiser for the foundation in Seattle which my good friend Gwen was attending and able to get me a ticket for. I was living in New York so all I needed to do was get myself on a plane and the rest would be taken care of.

I had a slight problem though, I had to wear a neck brace/chest harness thing because I was still fresh out of surgery. I didn't think that much of it at the time, but my doctor had a very different opinion. There was no chance in hell I was going to be allowed to fly across the country in the condition I was in. Simply put, I was not going to Seattle, was not attending the charity luncheon, was not going to meet Mike McCready. I didn't think I could hate this surgery any more than I already did, but alas, the hate grew to infinite proportions.

Before the news of not being allowed to go to Seattle, I couldn't wait for the day of the event. Now that I knew I wasn't going to be there, I wanted to sleep the day away and just move on with my life. I was beyond disappointed. With my hopes of unconsciousness not being realized, I was trying to pass the time in any way I could. As I was bumming around my house when the day I now dreaded had finally arrived, my phone suddenly rang. I looked at it and it was Gwen. Not really in the mood to hear about what a great time was being had by all in attendance or that Mike had decided to eat at the table I was supposed to be at, I contemplated not answering the call. As it turned out, that would have been a mistake.

I reluctantly answered the phone with a half-hearted, "Hey, Gwen," hoping she'd pick up on my malaise and temper her excitement as she updated me on all that I was missing, misery does love company after all.

"Is this Rob?" a man's voice cautiously asked. I confirmed to myself and aloud that yes, I am named Rob, and the caller continued, "Hey bud, it's Mike McCready."

Ok, so now I must determine, within milliseconds, if this was indeed Michael David McCready, guitar god from one of my favorite bands, Pearl Jam, or a very insensitive prank concocted by Gwen. I immediately decided that a) Gwen would never do such a thing and b) from the interviews I'd heard over the previous fourteen or fifteen years, the voice on the other end of the phone did sound familiar.

"Hey, Mike," I muttered as if we'd been next-door neighbors for decades. I'd be lying if I said that I remember the entire conversation, word for word, but I remember the topics, tone, and vibe of the nearly ten-minute call. A call I would have never guessed I'd receive, ever.

On what was a very big day for Mike, he took the time to call a stranger who he was told was a very big fan of his band and had planned to fly to Seattle for the fundraiser until spine surgery got in the way. That was, and still is, shocking to me. Maybe it's because we put those we look up to on pedestals too often and forget they're just human beings like the rest of us. Maybe it's because in Mike's case, he has provided me, along with millions of other fans,

CHAPTER 1: THE CONNECTION: FEELING MUSIC AND ITS LASTING EFFECTS

countless hours of soul-saving music, both live and recorded, and we can't possibly comprehend him calling us on the phone. Either way, on a day like this one, he certainly did not have to take the time to call some fan in New York whom he did not know and would likely never know just to thank him for a trip he never made.

That human connection I was referring to a few paragraphs ago is perfectly described in this ten-minute interaction I had with Mike McCready. Music connects people in ways other art forms seemingly do not. If you learn that someone you know is a fan of the same bands or genres of music that you are, there is an immediate bond. Does it mean you will become best friends? Not always, no. But a connection was made and regardless of the type of interaction you share with that person going forward, you will always have that bond, that connection. It can work from fan to artist and artist to fan as shown in my story about McCready's phone call. In this case, Pearl Jam had built a solid reputation for treating their fans with dignity, care, and respect since they burst onto the musical landscape in the early '90s, and McCready's actions proved that philosophy was alive and well with me in 2005.

When you break it all down, this book is about the connection the music of the early '90s had on the fans and musicians themselves who were experiencing and making it over three decades ago. There's a term described by Dr. Jakubowski called the "Reminiscence Bump," which is the tendency for older adults (typically over forty) to have increased or enhanced recollection of events that occurred during adolescence and early childhood. So, there's a bigger picture here. That picture can only now be seen with the help of science, history, time, and hindsight. It's true that the grunge or alternative era eventually faded from the charts and new genres would come to reign supreme. That is typical in culture and the music business overall. Perhaps the fact that its hold over popular culture did come to an end is a big testament to the bigger picture the book is about.

See, the music of the early '90s to mid-'90s never went away as the charts and record sales may have implied. It simply shifted from pop culture toward the countless millions who incorporated it into their daily lives and used it as some sort of sonic conductor to help guide them through the next phases of their lives. That's why it has lived for so long. That's why people who are in their fifties today have introduced it to their kids who are now starting to gain an appreciation and understanding of what happened over thirty years ago. It is why you can pick your children up from their grammar, middle, or high schools, and see numerous kids in Nirvana shirts. It's why Olivia Rodrigo has covered songs at her live shows by '90s bands such as Veruca Salt, No Doubt, and Republica.

Like the British Invasion had done in the 1960s, the grunge and alternative movement of the early and mid-'90s created the foundation that generations to follow would be built on. It was more than music, fashion, and the "flavor of the month." It was, and still is, a mindset, a personal culture, and a way of life. Certain music, at specific moments in time, wields power that goes far beyond the drums, guitars, bass, and vocals coming from our speakers. Music can create a generation. It's a power that is difficult to explain yet impossible not to feel. I believe that music has long-lasting effects. Actually, I know it does.

CHAPTER 2 – 1984
THE INFLUENCE BEGINS: BENEATH THE FAÇADE OF BUBBLE GUM, THE ROOTS OF GRUNGE GROW

"I DON'T WANT TO LIVE ANYMORE," I SAID TO MY MOTHER IN THE UPSTAIRS BATHROOM OF OUR house in Brooklyn. "I'm not happy," slipped out of my mouth as the only follow-up I could muster. It was 1982 and I was nine years old.

Turning her head quickly to the left, she held it there for what seemed like hours before, not so calmly saying, "What did you say?"

The rest of the conversation was fuzzy, but I remember not talking all that much anyway. As a parent now, I cannot fathom hearing a statement like that from one of my children. I don't know what I'd think or do. That's the burden I put on my mom though. A single parent, in her mid-thirties, raising two children under the age of ten alone because her husband left her four years earlier, and now had to suddenly deal with a suicidal toddler. She'd hear these words from me again, almost two decades later.

By all accounts, I was a very outgoing and talkative child. I never missed an opportunity to tell someone how I was feeling, why I felt that way, and what I was probably going to feel like soon. I was happy and had a big personality. I wasn't shy and had an opinion on everything. My mom jokes to this day that instead of "mama" or "mommy" as my first word, it was "why."

From the earliest days of my life up until that shocking conversation in the bathroom in Brooklyn, I was a very happy child. Or so it seemed. After my confession about my feelings toward living beyond nine, my mother had me see a therapist which I did for about a year. This was the start of my on-again, off-again relationship with therapy.

Now fast forward, and it's early December 2022. I'm sitting in a great local coffee shop called Main Street Coffee, in Staten Island, New York, writing this book about music that began over thirty years ago listening to twenty-something-year-olds discuss Rage Against the Machine, Streetlife Manifesto, Ska and Punk music. Talk about serendipity! They have no idea that I'm just a few feet away, writing about the very music and time they're discussing, and they have no idea that the fact that they're discussing this music at all, is proof that the influence of that period and those musical genres is still quite relevant. These kids showed up to work today thinking they'd make coffee, serve food, and listen to music and meanwhile, they've unknowingly become case studies for my book.

Almost without missing a beat, "Touch Me I'm Sick" by Mudhoney comes on over their sound system and suddenly I'm not sure what year it is inside this place, but I love it.

When I was in my late teens and early twenties, we didn't have the coffee house culture that we do now. I do remember though that I gathered with my music-loving friends in the non-sorority/frat cafeteria (can you say outcasts?) at St. John's University in Staten Island, New York affectionately known as "*The Rat.*" That's where a small but passionate group of metal, punk, rap, alternative, and grunge fans would gather to discuss the music they loved while sharing a campus, mostly made up of pop and dance music fans. We were the punks, the loners, the long hairs, and the outsiders. It's exactly where we belonged. It was 1991, I was a freshman in college and alternative rock, later to be known the world over, as grunge, was bubbling up from the underground

CHAPTER 2 - 1984: THE INFLUENCE BEGINS

music scene in Seattle, Washington. The story of that music, the music that would soon be everywhere, did not begin in 1991, however, not even close.

There was a slew of bands, some from the Seattle area, and some who weren't, that influenced the bands that would become grunge. We could go all the way back to '60s garage rock to bands like The Sonics and The Wailers (not the Bob Marley Wailers), early '70s glam such as T. Rex, Roxy Music, David Bowie, and The New York Dolls and the mid-'70s punk with such examples as The Ramones, The Clash, The Wipers, and Buzzcocks. Some of these bands, although they were around first, would experience their greatest success once the artists they influenced in Seattle broke out, including the '80s bands listed below. The '80s was largely known for bubble gum pop music, but beneath that façade, the grunge roots ran deep.

Bands like The Replacements, Pixies, U2, R.E.M., The Jesus and Mary Chain, The Stone Roses, Violent Femmes, Sonic Youth, XTC, Faith No More, Red Hot Chili Peppers, Jane's Addiction, Husker Du, etc. all had varying degrees of success or at least music industry notoriety before the '90s. All of them, however, would realize much greater fame once the music they helped pave the way for exploded on a global level, starting with the meteoric rise of Nirvana's first single, "Smells Like Teen Spirit" off their second album, *Nevermind*, 1991.

Popular music scenes don't usually fall from the sky. Most genres will borrow from what came before, add a few tweaks here and there, put a different spin onto a sound, and sometimes when the stars align, a massive musical movement is born. Nirvana didn't blow up strictly out of the blue. They weren't a happy little accident without a lineage. Their astronomical success, which still lives to this day may not have been forecast, but their sound and style had been brewing for years, tucked neatly into the dark, rainy underground of Seattle's rock music scene.

There are arguments to be made and discussions to have regarding the band or artist that started what would become grunge and those are always fun to have. In my opinion, due to when this band came out, and the bands it would eventually split into, I've always considered Green River to be "patient zero" when it comes to grunge music. Depending on who you're talking to, you will hear it was the Melvins, Malfunkshun, The U-Men, Bam Bam, Skin Yard, or the aforementioned, Green River and honestly, all have a reasonable claim to the title of the first grunge band.

Green River formed in Seattle in 1984 with singer Mark Arm, guitarist Steve Turner, bassist Jeff Ament, drummer Alex Vincent, and a little bit later, guitarist Stone Gossard. The band would record their first demo in June of 84 and by December of that year, they would start work on their first EP, *Come On Down*, for Long Island, New York's Homestead Records. As grunge would later be described as a mixture of punk rock and heavy metal, *Come On Down*, certainly falls into that description. Some of the early Seattle bands were combining hardcore punk with metal as well, and lines in the sand were being drawn as to who was more "metal" and who was more "punk/hardcore," which would ultimately dictate which way most musicians would go creatively.

This split in direction would affect Green River very early on in its career as original guitarist Steve Turner was unhappy with the heavy metal leanings of Gossard and Ament and quit the band once they'd wrapped up production on the EP in the middle of 1985. The record would be released in November of 85, almost a year after the initial recording process began. There wasn't a lot of buzz surrounding *Come On Down* and record sales were lacking because of it. Despite the lackluster release, *Come On Down* would ultimately be viewed by many as the first "grunge" record as it predated both the Melvins self-titled debut EP and the *Deep Six* compilation by C/Z Records which featured six Seattle bands who would soon be known as some of the early forefathers of the grunge movement. The bands included in this landmark compilation

CHAPTER 2 - 1984: THE INFLUENCE BEGINS

were: Soundgarden, Melvins, Skin Yard, The U-Men, Malfunkshun, and Green River.

After Turner's departure, a former bandmate of Jeff Ament's, Bruce Fairweather, from his previous band, Deranged Diction, joined Green River on guitar to replace Turner. The new lineup would begin work on their follow-up to *Come On Down* with a new EP titled, *Dry as a Bone* but this release wouldn't see the light of day for a few years. The story of Green River does not end here as what would come of them very shortly would lay the foundation for one of the biggest bands in the history of American rock music.

As I mentioned, the '80s was, on the surface, a time of pop music. 1984 was not known for grunge or alternative music by any stretch of the imagination. As a matter of fact, outside of Seattle, most people around the country did not know who Green River was, what Sub Pop was, or that anything but pop music was being played on radios around the country. Pop icon Michael Jackson won a record eight Grammy awards in 1984, proving just how dominant pop music was during that time. There has always been an underground when it comes to music. It was happening in big cities like New York, Chicago, and Los Angeles, as well as smaller towns like Athens, Georgia, Minneapolis, Minnesota, Austin, Texas, and yes, Seattle, Washington.

The rest of the country though, was groovin' to "What's Love Got To With It" by Tina Turner, "Footloose" by Kenny Loggins, "Hello" by Lionel Richie, and "Thriller" by Michael Jackson. There were some rock songs on the charts as well like "Jump" by Van Halen, "Owner of a Lonely Heart" by Yes, *and* "Eyes Without a Face" by Billy Idol, amongst others, but nothing remotely close to what the underground was producing then. The country wasn't ready for that.

Western culture during the 1980s was somewhat of a conservative reaction to the free-loving liberal ideals of the '60s and '70s. Ronald Regan became President of the United States in 1981 and served two full terms ending in 1989. His English counterpart, the leader of the Conservative Party in England since 1975, Margaret Thatcher, became the Prime Minister of the United Kingdom in 1979 ruling through 1990. The '80s have been dubbed the decade of materialism and consumerism by many who lived through it, despite suffering two recessions at the very start of the decade. The US economy recovered quite nicely from 1982-1990 with a growth rate of over 37 percent. In other words, things were going well, and the powers that be didn't want anything or anyone to rock the proverbial boat.

Conservative politics, a strong middle and upper class, and a society hellbent on spending their money shopping at the mall can make some people content and satisfied. The phrase "art imitates life" can be accurately used to describe what was big on Top 40 radio and MTV during most of the '80s. The sound and lyrics of the most popular songs were safe, upbeat, and centered around love, happiness, parties, and the like. I've heard many artists say that inspiration often comes from difficult times. The '80s, on the surface, seemed anything but difficult. It was prosperous in ways the country had only seen a few times before. Below the surface, however, many people, me included, were not so cheery. I was eleven years old in '84 and had already been in therapy because just a few short years earlier, I wanted to die. Songs like "Say, Say, Say" (Paul McCartney and Michael Jackson), "Ghostbusters" (Ray Parker Jr.), and "Karma Chameleon" (Culture Club), which were all included in *the Billboard Year-End Hot 100 Singles of 1984* weren't exactly doing it for me. It appears I wasn't alone as 1984 was also the year that the underground in Seattle got going. A revolution was brewing, and I was, albeit unknowingly, a part of it.

At this point, my limited cassette and vinyl collection consisted of albums by Led Zeppelin, Black Sabbath, Iron Maiden, Def Leppard, Quiet Riot, David Bowie, and The Police. I wasn't allowed to publicly announce this, but I also liked Prince, Duran Duran, The Ramones, The Clash, and U2. Back in those days, you had to declare the music you liked, and with Iron Maiden's

CHAPTER 2 – 1984: THE INFLUENCE BEGINS

cover art from their 1983 album *Piece of Mind*, proudly covering the back of my denim jacket, I was a metalhead, case closed. Luckily this closed-minded approach to music fandom would one day fade, but the early '80s wasn't that time, at least not on a large scale anyway. I didn't know it then, but the heavy riffs and dark themes I was attracted to from bands like Sabbath and Maiden, combined with the catchy punk stylings of The Ramones and early records from The Police, along with the New Wave of Duran Duran and soon to be discovered (for me anyway) R.E.M., and Sonic Youth, the seeds of something new were being sewn into the musical garden just beginning to grow inside of me.

Culturally, the United States was navigating itself through the middle of a new decade, still trying to recover from the chaos of its 1970s hangover. Republican Ronald Reagan was in his first of two terms in The White House, and the country was leaning conservative, both socially and politically. The Cold War was still raging and as a show of defiance and aggression, the Soviet Union refused to participate in the 1984 Olympics held in Los Angeles, California. The AIDS epidemic was at its peak and scientists had announced the cause of the deadly disease, a retrovirus they called HIV (Human Immunodeficiency Virus), and panic rose to epic levels. Times like these have long been the starting point for new and aggressive art to emerge.

When people get angry, confused, scared, or fed up, sometimes they combat those feelings with an outpouring of artistic energy. It doesn't always happen immediately though. People need to first become motivated by what's going on around them and then figure out a way to present that motivation to the rest of the world. So, for the time being, as those thoughts and ideas were beginning to flow to future artists, the pop music and culture of the day would suffice as an escape. In the entertainment world, commercial music, as discussed earlier, was non-threatening and "safe."

Hollywood, never an entity to take chances, was pumping out ho-hum films such as *Ghostbusters*, *Gremlins*, *Footloose*, *Romancing the Stone*, and the like. These films were huge at the box office but offered little in the way of artistic influence. On the surface, life in America in 1984 was fine. But beneath the surface, unemployment was very high (over 7 percent), and urban crime across the country was reaching increasingly high levels, a music-loving 11-year-old such as myself was content in my bedroom with my records, headphones, and rock 'n' roll magazines. Something was brewing though and on a subconscious level, I felt it. The music that grabbed a hold of me and infiltrated the nooks and crannies of my imagination was more than just loud sounds the adults in my life didn't understand. There was a deeper connection here.

Writing *SLACKER* goes beyond describing the genre and period of music I love the most. It's also a way to explore the psychology of how and why certain types of music and/or bands and artists can resonate with more people than other genres or scenes. There can be no argument that the explosion of rock 'n' roll in the early and mid-'50s was one of, if not the first, music scene to embed itself into the psyche of young people and cause a commotion that is still felt to this day. Same goes for the British invasion of the early 1960s, the hippie movement of the late '60s/early '70s, the New York punk rock scene of the mid-1970s which would make its way across the Atlantic Ocean to England and back again, and a bit later, the commercialization of a new genre in the early/mid-'80s, hip-hop. Looking back at all the influence the music I just described has had on modern culture, I must look no further than the fashion and lifestyles these genres created, which still have relevance today.

Can anyone wiggle their hips and sneer on stage and not see be compared to Elvis, even facetiously? When was the last time you attended a Halloween party and did not see at least one Hippie there? The Beatles are still one of the most popular bands on planet Earth and they broke up in 1970. The Rolling Stones are still touring so the '60s have had a lasting and highly influential presence for decades.

CHAPTER 2 - 1984: THE INFLUENCE BEGINS

Punk and hip-hop were mirror images of one another at the time in terms of music and lyrics from the street. Both dealt with the underserved communities in their respective cultures and the music was loud, abrasive, and unapologetic. Punk and hip-hop have gone on to iconic heights that were never predicted when they both began and continue to defy the odds today. Of course, there were and are other types of music, scenes, and pop culture takeovers, but for the most part, the ones mentioned here seemed to have had the biggest societal impact.

The early '90s Seattle scene, which spawned grunge and helped elevate the already underway alternative scene into the stratosphere, would be next in line after the ascension of hip-hop. But that scene didn't materialize out of thin air. Nirvana didn't create *Nevermind* in a vacuum and surprised the music industry with its sound and style. Things had been cooking for quite some time before 1991.

To get some perspective on what I think is the closest cultural music movement to the grunge era, I sought the wisdom of Sociologist, PhD, writer, Ramones aficionado, and overall music and culture badass, Dr. Donna Gaines. Dr. Gaines' work can be seen in the likes of *Rolling Stone*, *Spin*, *The Village Voice*, and *Salon*, as well as numerous scholarly collections, professional journals, and textbooks. In addition to those credentials, Dr. Gaines has published several books including *Teenage Wasteland: Suburbia's Dead End Kids, A Misfits Manifesto*, and the book I wanted to talk with her about the most, *Why The Ramones Matter*.

I was born in 1973, so I was too young to witness the rise of punk rock, which many believe was created by the unlikely band of outcasts from Queens, New York, The Ramones. I'd come to learn of and love the band in the mid/late '80s, but by then the world had already fallen in love with a band that didn't like one another yet somehow created a sound, scene, and movement that the entire world would copy and benefit from. What does one do when they aren't around to witness something themself? They go and find someone who was and in the case of Donna Gaines, few people had a better view of or connection with the band than she had. Seeing as how Dr. Gaines was front and center for one of the biggest music movements with a profound impact on culture, punk in the mid-'70s, I wanted her perspective on a myriad of topics related to the early '90s grunge movement.

"When it comes to the creation of new genres of music," Dr. Gaines says. "It's not just the music. It's the look, it also must have a philosophical base, a distinctive sound or feel, a lineage, and having a regional element to it all is huge."

This was the case with The Ramones, and it certainly was the case with the early grunge and alternative bands hailing from Seattle in the early 1980s. I was looking for a bridge, some connective tissue to link what happened with punk in the '70s and marry it with the grunge explosion.

I'm convinced that you always need to look back to understand the present and Dr. Gaines provided a plausible connection, "Around 1992, there was a sea change, a cultural shift. People were ready for something different. College radio had a lot to do with it. There was also a class difference. To me, the real link was CJ Ramone because he's a part of Generation X. He brought in new blood for the Ramones and the bands from the Pacific Northwest have always acknowledged the Ramones as the godfathers of the music they were influenced by."

I can't help but think of the irony that existed in 1984 between the slow death of the punk rock scene and the start of what would become the global behemoth known as grunge. Just when the Ramones were at their lowest point commercially as their 1984 album, *Too Tough to Die* became the band's lowest peaking record at that point in their career (171 on the US Billboard 200 chart), Green River was planting the seeds for the movement that was going to take over where punk and the Ramones left off. And with society dealing with bigger problems, escapism in music was starting to feel just plain fake.

CHAPTER 2 – 1984: THE INFLUENCE BEGINS

I suppose I was destined to be the type of person who thought deeply about what I was feeling and analyzed everything I'd encountered in life. It makes sense now, with age and hopefully some wisdom behind me, but back then I just wanted to be a kid. I loved sports, music, and hanging out with my friends. My family life was fine I guess, but it was hectic. Without a dad at home and a mom who was always working, I had a lot of time to wonder about life and come up with answers on my own that I probably needed to get from the adults who should have been around me. It didn't work out that way though and I had to forge my path. Carving a lane out for the road I'd travel on at eleven was a daunting and unfortunate task, but what choice did I have? Well, I did have one place to go when I needed or wanted guidance, I wasn't getting anywhere else.

The walls of my bedroom were covered in posters and magazine tear-outs featuring the likes of Black Sabbath, Iron Maiden, Led Zeppelin, The Beatles, and Def Leppard, along with a handful of Yankees and Jets players for good measure. My headphones, dual cassette boombox, and record player were my escapes. As much as I was looking to get out of my head once I'd press "play," I know now I was also seeking knowledge. Kids tend to look to adults, known to them or not, to teach them . . . everything. Most kids get that from their parents, grandparents, or teachers. I got it from Robert Plant, Bruce Dickinson, and Ozzy Osbourne. Again, I will not pretend that I knew what I was doing or even looking for in my adolescence when it came to guidance and knowledge, but I do know music was always there for me when I needed it to be. It still is. I've always been extremely curious about everything in life, and I want to understand the "why" in it all.

In trying to figure out the "why" in everything, I reached out to Joseph J. Williams, Licensed Mental Health Counselor, Cognitive Behavioral Therapist, and Associate Fellow at the Albert Ellis Institute, for his thoughts on what role music can play in the lives of young people as it concerns their worldview and how they navigate their lives.

Williams said, "If their parents had a strong influence on their view of the world, that might be the foundation. If they didn't, it might be music. As kids get older, parental influence is less. Music can also sustain a worldview they've already had."

It's fascinating to me how words, sung over rhythms and beats that seep into our subconscious, can become part of the foundation, the very fabric of who we are. The connection, and more importantly, the impact that all aspects of music can have on us is something that is being studied more and more as time goes on. For Baby Boomers looking back on the '50s and '60s, or Gen Xers feeling the '80s and '90s, these connections, like them or not, have helped shape who we are as individuals and as a society. The components that bind these facts together, like the pieces needed to construct a model train, are strongest when we're young.

I can honestly say that my coming-of-age moments, whether political, cultural, or personal, all have music attached to them or were developed in part by what I learned and felt through music. Song lyrics from some of my favorite artists would prompt me to learn about the subject matter they were writing about and help shape my view at times. Did this mean I'd follow along blindly and agree with everything they said? Not at all. What it did though was open my eyes and mind to things I knew little about or it allowed me to look at something I was aware of through a different lens. Whether introspective topics such as depression and mental health or global issues like war or famine, were coming through my speakers, I was more acutely in tune with them than I was before, and they helped guide me to a path of understanding.

"Age matters. When you're young, there's less in the way, less clutter. If you're 29 and first hearing new music, there are already filters that distract messages. Younger kids may have a more honest interpretation," explains Williams when discussing the role that age, as well as cultural factors, can play in the attachment and weight that music will have in the long term.

CHAPTER 2 - 1984: THE INFLUENCE BEGINS

As Green River, unbeknownst to them at the time, was busy laying the foundation for what would become a new musical genre and eventually a worldwide phenomenon, another group of Seattle musicians were gearing up to join them. With the breakup of the local Seattle band, the Shemps, which bassist Hiro Yamamoto and singer/drummer Chris Cornell were both in, (Yamamoto was later replaced on bass by Kim Thayil) the seeds for a new band were beginning to grow. Yamamoto eventually reunited with Cornell for a post-Shemps project, and along with Thayil, the trio would form Soundgarden. Thayil would relinquish bass duties back to Yamamoto and become the new band's guitarist, with Cornell remaining on vocals and drums. By 1985 though, the band realized Cornell's true calling was to be freed from the drum kit and focus on singing. The band wouldn't officially release anything until 1988. I'll talk about that a bit later in the book, but I wanted to bring up the birth of Soundgarden because it happened in the same year that Green River would get its start, linking the bands forever as two of the earliest and most important figures in the history of grunge.

1984, in my opinion, is the year where the discussion of what would become the grunge movement in Seattle should start, even though a few bands, like some on the *Deep Six* compilation mentioned earlier, had started before 1984. Andrew Wood's (later of Mother Love Bone) band Malfunkshun started in 1980, as did The U-Men. 1983 saw the creation of the Melvins and Bam Bam (featuring Matt Cameron who would eventually drum for Soundgarden, Temple of the Dog, and Pearl Jam) who would both have a profound effect on the entire scene. It's entirely plausible that with the Melvins, Nirvana would have never been noticed by anyone outside of Aberdeen, Washington, or worse yet, not have existed at all. The incubation period for grunge was from 1980-1984 and some of the musicians from those bands who are responsible for the start and direction of the scene, are still going strong today. Four decades later, even longer when you include the earliest influences from '60s garage rock and '70s metal and punk, you can easily look back and see why this genre has the legs and longevity that most musical movements simply never attain.

Before the digital age, music scenes began with people who desired to play music in a room with other people. Laptop computers and music-making software did not exist. The sheer love of music and the unstoppable drive to feel a part of something drove people to create. Musicians couldn't develop scenes alone. They may have been the catalysts, but they needed help. They needed people to listen to their songs, audiences to attend their shows, writers, and photographers to document what was happening, and promoters and clubs to push and showcase the talent. Local radio and TV stations would come into play as would mom-and-pop record stores and indie record labels. If done correctly, with sheer grit, determination, talent, and a few lucky breaks, a culture, and a scene would spring up and it was all because music brings people together.

I interviewed Jared Miller, a club promoter, artist manager, and photographer from New York. He is a great example of someone who intuitively knew he was meant to be involved in and a part of a music scene.

"I was a music fanatic and started bringing cameras to shows when I was 17. Then in 1983, I was a freshman at NYU (New York University), and living down the hall from me was a junior named Rick Rubin. He and I became friends because he was in a band called Hose and his bass player was my older brother's roommate. Rick got me a job working with him at the front desk of the dormitory at Weinstein Hall. From midnight to 9 AM we'd listen to music and hangout with LL Cool J and the Beastie Boys. I kind of saw the birth of Def Jam."

This is just one of the reasons I loved the era before digital music took over. Stories like Jared's were common in the fact that it was completely reasonable, and even likely, that if you showed interest in the local music scene you'd run into, meet, and probably work with the musicians that would go on to make the scene a hit. Jared's career arc in the music industry is a shin-

CHAPTER 2 - 1984: THE INFLUENCE BEGINS

ing example of how you could become what you wanted to become if you went for it. As Jared and I continued our conversation, this philosophy would prove fruitful at just the right time to wind up as a player in the grunge and alternative world.

"I moved to L.A. in 1987," Miller continued, "with the intention of getting into the music industry. I'd go to clubs every night and go up to bands asking if they needed a manager. Eventually, bands would start letting me help, not as a manager, but help with flyers, promotion, and everything else. I became immersed in that world and learned everything I could about the business. In 1991, I moved back to NY and hooked up with a guy who was booking a bar called Desmond's Tavern, his name was Johnny Jones. With my business sense and his social butterflyness, we started taking over clubs and bars as promoters. In addition to Desmond's, we booked for Sun Mountain Cafe, Nevada Smiths, The Lion's Den, and later we were promoters for Danceteria, Limelight, Club USA, and The Tunnel. In 1993-1994 I became a house photographer for CBGB's."

The more Jared and I spoke, the more his story resonated with me. We're from the same generation, fell in love with the same music around the same time, and I know for a fact that I attended some of the shows he booked and promoted based on the timelines. When I speak about a local, physical, pre-digital age music scene, this is how it was done. Times have changed and there are new ways to break bands and artists but trust me, it's nothing like how it was in the mid and late '80s.

Creating a music culture in this fashion was something that, even if it flew under the radar, we all felt an emotional attachment to and bonded over. Going to clubs like L'Amour, in Brooklyn in the late '80s and then venues like The Wave and Rock Palace in Staten Island during the early and mid-'90s, to see metal, hardcore, punk, and alternative music was the norm for a music lover like me. Neighborhoods covered with handmade flyers printed at Kinko's and passed out after "big" shows at theatre-sized venues in Manhattan (frequently you'd get a cassette tape or CD of the band that was being promoted on the flyer) were how we knew where to go and when to show up. This was how scenes were created. To be in the know, you had to be at the show. This was nothing new however, it was just the scene I was old enough to be a part of.

Before my time, mainly during the early and mid-'70s, New York clubs like CBGB helped cultivate artists like the Ramones, Television, Blondie, Patti Smith, Talking Heads, and countless others because some people (in this case, CBGB owner, Hilly Kristol) had enough vision and taste to understand that all types of music needed exposure to flourish. The commercial radio stations and mainstream media weren't interested in taking chances on unknown commodities. Thankfully, Hilly was. Once again though, this sort of forward-thinking and chance-taking wasn't new. A decade or two before the art and punk scene happened at CBGB, a folk revival was occurring in the city that never sleeps. With the help of places like the Gaslight Café, Folkways Records, WNYC Radio, Washington Square Park, and other entities that allowed and encouraged artistic expression, artists such as Woodie Guthrie, Lead Belly, Pete Seeger, Bob Dylan, and more gained national and global stardom.

Learning the history of the music scenes before my own through books, magazines, and documentaries, along with some older people in my life recounting their experiences in it, I felt a kinship toward those who lived in and operated the scenes before me. Because of that, I felt something was starting to brew for the music I was falling in love with then, at least in and around New York City, and I knew I'd be a part of that. The scene that was getting ready to take over lent itself to the old-school, and somewhat forgotten punk ethos of the DIY (Do It Yourself) movement of days gone by. The backlash to pop music was beginning, and although grunge was virtually unknown to the world outside of Seattle, the need for deeper music to give us something to hold on to was starting to take hold.

CHAPTER 3 – 1985
CONCERTS AND FUNDRAISERS:
THE POWER OF PEOPLE COMING TOGETHER THROUGH MUSIC

"YOU GUYS WANT SOME?" LOOKING OVER MY SHOULDER, PAST MY DAD, I SAW A MAN WHO was probably in his late 20s or early 30s, long hair covering his face as if he was hiding from the rest of the world, holding open a clear freezer bag, maybe a quart-sized one, full of drugs. "Take whatever you want," slurred the wannabe pharmacist we were lucky enough to be sitting next to at the Nassau Veterans Memorial Coliseum watching Iron Maiden bring the house down during their 1985 Powerslave tour.

Being just twelve years old and sitting next to my dad, I wasn't about to say a word to the guy. I looked at him briefly, then turned back toward my friend Jimmy to continue our synchronized headbanging routine to the blaring heavy metal directed right to our faces from the stage.

I remember my dad shaking his head in disgust at the very generous illegal drug offer and muttering something to the effect of "What's the matter with you? I've got kids here." On the drive home, we didn't speak of the incident. My dad and I never did things like this, so it was a little awkward to begin with. He wasn't a fan of heavy metal and probably hated the concert, but I begged him to take me because I was too young to go on my own. Since my parents' divorce in 1978, my relationship with my dad had become strained so I guess neither of us knew what to say regarding this odd, yet teachable moment. Being on the same page with him, or even having meaningful conversations were infrequent and this would only progress in the years to come.

I couldn't believe my luck. I was seeing Iron Maiden live in concert! To say that this was the best news that twelve-year-old me would have received is an understatement of gigantic proportions. This wouldn't be my first time seeing live music, mind you. A year earlier, I had the pleasure and good fortune of seeing New Wave sensation, Duran Duran at the Nassau Coliseum in Uniondale, New York, a suburb of Nassau County in the town of Hempstead on Long Island. Not only did I see the band responsible for such huge radio hits (and videos) as "Girls on Film," "Rio," "Hungry Like the Wolf," "Save a Prayer," and "The Reflex," but I arrived in style with some friends in a white limousine.

I feel an explanation is in order. During the 1980s, I became more and more curious regarding the styles of music I wanted to explore. Still a big fan of heavy metal, I slowly started diving into punk rock, New Wave, some pop, and by the mid-80s, rap. For those of you who didn't grow up in the '80s, there was this strange, yet genuine rule you had to follow as a music fan: if you liked a certain genre of music, that was it. That's what you had to listen to. You couldn't like metal and pop, punk and disco. It wasn't "allowed" by the musical guardians of integrity. Or more appropriately, the older, pot-smoking siblings of your friends, who as it turns out, had no idea what they were talking about. At the time though, it was quite real.

In some walks of life, the music you listen to could brand you as an outcast, barely tolerated in society. Included in this branding was how you dressed. I had the denim jacket and patches, the necessary uniform to be classified as a "metalhead". The biggest declaration you had to make was who was going to be on the back of the jacket, as I briefly mentioned earlier in the book. The front didn't matter as much. You could have patches and pins of

CHAPTER 3 – 1985: CONCERTS AND FUNDRAISERS

all the bands you like. The back, however, that was the shit! Whoever was on the back was the best band in the world and no one could tell you differently (more on this in a bit).

There were secondary rules as well. During my metal years and denim jacket fashion, there were rifts within the same headbanging community. Maiden fans had an enemy. Judas Priest was another massively popular metal band from that era, and like party lines in politics, you had to choose who you rocked with. If you were a Maiden fan, you had to denounce Priest, or at least put them below Maiden. That's just how it was back then. On the surface, in front of friends and strangers, you had to operate within the rigidity of those rules. At home, however, within the confines and safety of the four walls of your poster-laden bedroom, you could (and did) listen to anything you'd like.

Although I was a self-proclaimed "metal-head" whose allegiance was to the headbanging nation of other metalheads the world over, or at least Brooklyn, I secretly like other genres of music. It's hard to be a music fan, especially a young one, and not find the catchy, upbeat melodies and sing-along choruses of Duran Duran irresistible. As for the limo, I had two rich friends as a kid, a brother and sister combo who lived around the block from me and the luxurious transportation choice was all theirs, I was just along for the ride, literally.

When that fateful day of the Iron Maiden concert finally came, and I was in the same building as my heavy metal heroes, I knew then that music, in one form or another, was to be my calling. I wanted to become a bass player like Maiden's fast-fingered founder and main songwriter, Steve Harris. It wasn't long after this show that my mom finally relented and signed me up for bass lessons. Whether it be as a musician, record label executive, writer, or even a radio DJ, I knew that my passion was soaked in music, and I needed a way to express that. Growing up in a single parent, working-class family, with a history of high school dropouts and city workers, dreaming of a career as a musician or anything related to the music industry was about as possible as becoming an astronaut. No one that I knew in real life had the slightest clue as to how to go after and capture a music career. Even though I was close enough to practically reach out and touch the god-like figures in Iron Maiden that night at the Nassau Coliseum, I was about as far away from leading a similar life to theirs as one could be.

In addition to Iron Maiden, I was also lucky enough to see Prince live in concert in 1985. Again, a full-on metal head seeing the "purple one" wasn't exactly what one would do back then if you wanted to keep your heavy metal fandom in good standing. In hindsight, I was always interested in many genres of music. The first music I remember hearing was the pop and rock songs of the '50s and '60s my mom would play on her favorite radio stations at home or the Doo-wop music I'd hear at family parties at various aunts and uncle's houses. From there it would be Motown and even some folk and singer/songwriter stuff from the '70s.

But heavy metal was mine. It was the first genre I identified with all on my own so the prospect of turning in my metal membership card just because I liked Prince and went to see him perform live wasn't something I was interested in doing. It's funny because, by the time grunge exploded in the early '90s, the genre it destroyed or at least removed from the public consciousness was metal. This was obviously unknown to the world in 1985, but the chains were slowly breaking and would completely shatter a few years later.

In Seattle, as Green River and Soundgarden were going about the business of creating something new, another local band, Screaming Trees, was recording its first EP, *Other Worlds*, in the summer of 1985. Sounding more like R.E.M. with Jim Morrison posthumously replacing Michael Stipe on lead vocals than the sludgy, punk of Green River, the band from Ellensburg, Washington was proof that the Seattle "sound" as it would come to be known later, really wasn't a sound at all. This is a topic that comes up frequently, but I think it's important to remind ourselves often that labels for popular music

CHAPTER 3 - 1985: CONCERTS AND FUNDRAISERS

are just that. They're labels. They're meant to identify artists of a specific time in history so it's easy to reference and have discussions about them more so than the need to be a sonic carbon copy.

Somewhere along the way, we've fallen into the trap that a label or "title" must correlate to a certain sound. Some think that anyone who's cast into the same net as someone else, tied together by a label, must sound alike. This isn't true. It doesn't have to be that way. Now, we must exercise a little logic and common sense here as well. Can we lump in Taylor Swift with Mozart? We cannot. So classical and pop musicians should remain separated.

That being said, the music of Screaming Trees and the music of Alice In Chains have many differences yet also have enough in common from a stylistic, geographical, time frame, and general attitude point of view, that they can absolutely be placed into the same genre even though the music isn't exactly the same. If you think about the Seattle bands that would break through commercially years later, Nirvana, Pearl Jam, Soundgarden, and Alice in Chains, they honestly don't sound like one another at all. They were from the same place, at the same time, and they did have a similar look by the time they were all on MTV, but musically they were vastly different. The idea that they sounded alike just isn't true. This divergence in sound was there from the start, and *Other Worlds* by Screaming Trees is proof of that.

Screaming Trees was another band that would ride the wave they helped create once the scene went global. The band, brothers Gary Lee (guitar) and Van Connor (bass), along with singer Mark Lanegan, and drummer Mark Pickerel was one of the first bands to be associated with the grunge movement even though they didn't have a sound that was anything like that of Green River or Soundgarden at that time. More jangly, melodic guitar rock than the brutal sludging of Green River or Soundgarden, Screaming Trees were easy to sing along to and built more for radio than the heavier sounds of the earliest grunge bands. Having Mark Lanegan as the lead singer though was enough to bring the weight and darkness to the lighter tones of the Trees' music. The band's biggest hit, "Nearly Lost You" off their 1992 album, *Sweet Oblivion*, (also included on the smash-hit soundtrack to the Cameron Crowe film, *Singles*) would put Screaming Trees on the grunge map for good. They would not reach the level of commercial success and notoriety again that they enjoyed after *Sweet Oblivion*, but their contribution to the scene cannot be diminished. Mark Lanegan would go on to have a very solid solo career, which began while still in Screaming Trees. He also enjoyed stints in Queens of the Stone Age, The Gutter Twins, and more, whose music was probably more in line with what people would describe as grunge than what the Screaming Trees were. Sadly, Lanegan and Van Connor would both die untimely deaths in 2022 and 2023 respectively.

Seattle wasn't the only West Coast city in the early and mid-'80s producing music that would take the world by storm in the '90s. Tucked away in the Echo Park neighborhood of Los Angeles, California, were two art/punk scene regulars named Donita Sparks and Suzi Gardner, who met through mutual friends in 1984. It was that meeting that would be the genesis of the band, L7. Eventually, the duo would enlist the help of Jennifer Finch on bass, and after a couple of drummers, Dee Plakas would join in late 1989 to form what would become the classic L7 lineup. What's important to recognize here is that while on the surface, far above the rock 'n' roll underground, commercial music didn't cater to punk or any form of heavy music that was either fronted by or consisting completely of women. L7 would find enough mainstream success, once the rules had all been broken in 1991, to help lead the charge of girls who could kick ass on their instruments, have something poetic and meaningful to say lyrically, and rock as hard as the boys.

Even those who didn't like the grunge movement would have to admit that it certainly opened the door a lot wider than it previously was for women to be involved in, and taken seriously, in the world of punk, alternative, and hardcore music. This wouldn't have been possible in the '90s if it wasn't for

CHAPTER 3 - 1985: CONCERTS AND FUNDRAISERS

trailblazing female artists like L7 to pave the way for not only themselves but also the other women who followed in their footsteps.

There was a major event that took place in 1985, meeting at the intersection of music and culture, that, at least in my young life, was the biggest musical event I'd ever seen. It was a single-day, multi-venue concert called Live Aid, and it was monstrous. Around Christmas of '84, a song called "Do They Know It's Christmas," written by musicians Bob Geldof and Midge Ure, was released as a charitable effort to combat a massive famine happening in Ethiopia. The song was performed by a "supergroup" put together by the songwriting duo, called Band Aid. The list of artists who made up Band Aid is too extensive to name but some musicians of note who performed on the record were: Bono, Boy George, Phil Collins, Simon Le Bon, George Michael, and Sting. In addition to the song itself, side two of the single contained spoken messages urging people to donate by stars such as David Bowie and Paul McCartney. Following the December 1984 release, and due in large part to its massive success, (the single reached a million copies sold in the first week, becoming the fastest-selling single in UK chart history), follow-up concerts were booked for the upcoming year. Those concerts, also conceived by Geldof and Ure, were dubbed Live Aid.

On July 13, 1985, over 161,000 people gathered in both Wembley Stadium (72K+) in London, England, and John F. Kennedy Stadium (89K +) in Philadelphia, PA in the United States to witness history. A total of 58 performances by some of the industry's biggest names, across both venues performed for an estimated 1.9 billion people worldwide. Approximately one-third of the global population had tuned into the broadcast at the same time. As I said, this was the biggest musical and cultural event I had ever seen. I'm willing to bet everyone else who watched it could say the same thing.

At twelve years old, I'm not sure how charitable I was but I did know why the concert was being held. I could empathize with people being hungry, especially since the tragic situation in Ethiopia was being broadcast on the nightly news in America, showing images of starving children almost around the clock. From 1983-1985, according to Worldvision.org and the United Nations, the food shortages and hunger crisis in Ethiopia led to an estimated one million famine-related deaths while leaving millions more displaced and left destitute. Experiencing recurring drought, failed harvests, food scarcity, and seemingly endless conflict that kept aid from reaching people in controlled territories, the situation was beyond bleak, and a tremendous humanitarian effort would be needed to save lives.

Looking back, of course, I realize how powerful advertising can be and at least in the case of Live Aid, it was used for a great cause. The undertaking of an event like this was massive. Organizing two concerts, on two separate continents and one hundred fifty nations, consisting of more than seventy artists and bands, playing over sixteen hours of music, in front of two gigantic live audiences (not to mention the nearly two billion watching on television), and using thirteen military satellites to transmit the whole thing . . . I'm exhausted just writing it, let alone thinking of how to pull it off.

But pull it off they did. Live Aid raised over forty million dollars on the day of the show (over one hundred million in today's money) and more than one hundred fifty million being raised overall. I'd be lying if I said I watched the event for any other reason than the music but the plight in Africa at the time did resonate with me, and I've since done what little I can for charitable causes. I did learn to appreciate what I have and help those in need, so music was once again acting as a mentor and a teacher. Learning that music and culture could and did collide for positive change was a good thing as it continued to set the table for what was to come in the following decade. Music, and the people in it, can do good if they choose.

On the flip side of culture, 1985 also taught me that things in America were perhaps too good for some folks. Most musical shifts or newly created genres happen when young people look around and don't like what they see. This is usually the case when the adults who wield power like parents, teach-

CHAPTER 3 - 1985: CONCERTS AND FUNDRAISERS

ers, politicians, and the media do things that kids vehemently disagree with and need to react in kind.

In April of 1985, the Coca-Cola Company launched a new version of, with a new recipe for, their classic soft drink, Coca-Cola. Unofficially dubbed, "New Coke," this new product hit the market and not long after, the chaos began. For a myriad of reasons, people didn't like this new flavor and instead of just not buying it, people lost their minds. The Coca-Cola Company received over 40,000 calls and letters of anger and disappointment. At one point, the company was fielding over 1,500 calls per day to its hotline when the average before the arrival of "New Coke" was about 400 per day. Coca-Cola even hired a psychiatrist to listen in on the calls they'd been receiving and told executives that some people sounded as if they were discussing the death of a family member.

I bring this story up as just one example of what might make kids look at the adults in the room and say, "really . . . all of this anger over soda?" I'd love to know how many kids threw their hands up in disgust around this time, picked up guitars, and started writing some heavy, angry, rock 'n' roll music. Punk rock, alternative, grunge, heavy metal, etc. typically started as a reaction by young, disaffected kids who could no longer relate to the bloated society they lived in and couldn't find solace in the music of the day.

According to Ycharts.com, an investment research firm, The Coca-Cola company's revenue in 1984 was over 7.3 billion dollars. Let me go out on a limb here and say that the soda pop king was doing just fine. The hysteria over the change in recipe was merely a blip on their cash-cow radar screen. It goes a little deeper than just money in my opinion. The optics and psychology of a company this large and successful in tricking people who work hard for a living, who exist in a world with so many real and significant problems losing their collective minds over the taste of soda were horrendous. The kids who were old enough to catch on must've been dumbfounded.

Could you imagine the not-so-made-up conversations taking place across the United States at this time? "Hey, Mom, can I talk to you, I'm feeling lonely and depressed and I'm not sure why."

The parent's reply would go something like this, "Not now son, they just changed the classic flavor of Coke, and I need to stay on hold with their helpline and get them to change it back before your father gets home. You know how much he likes his Coke with dinner!"

What the hell were kids supposed to do? The only thing they could. Rebel against this odd, out-of-touch behavior and write music to blow off steam. Think about how crazy this was. On the one hand, we were coming together in *Live Aid* to raise funds for starving children, and on the other hand, we were pitching a fit over a formula change for a soft drink.

Not only were the adults in my life crying about soda in 1985, but they were also upset about my appearance, along with my musical tastes. In my Catholic grammar school, the principal and some teachers did not like the heavy metal "look" which I was trying my best to emulate, so there was a consequence based on their dislike. I was given a week's detention, an archaic practice when an authority figure at school doesn't know how to handle a child who has done something wrong in their eyes, so they make that child sit in an empty classroom for an hour after school for a predetermined number of days. What was my heinous offense you ask? Well, at twelve years old and in the seventh grade, I had the nerve, the unmitigated gall, to wear a denim jacket with the cover art to Iron Maiden's 1983 album, *Piece of Mind*, pressed onto the back.

If you're unfamiliar with that album cover, it was a depiction of their mascot, a havoc-wreaking, back-from-the-dead, skeleton named Eddie, wearing a strait jacket, tied up in chains, and left to die in a rubber room. A bit morbid? Sure. A crime worth an hour of my time for five consecutive days after school, fuck no. At this point, the vanilla music being pumped through our radios and the fear of any music that sounded different from that music, accompanied by a "scary" look or fashion, needed to disappear.

CHAPTER 3 - 1985: CONCERTS AND FUNDRAISERS

So, at this time, in basements, garages, and cheap recording studios around the country, twenty-something-year-olds, fed up with what was happening musically and culturally around them, were writing the songs and inventing the genres that would soon tear at the very fabric of the safe, sterile, commercial music being force-fed to America's youth. And millions of young kids like me, not happy with life, struggling with issues and going to therapy, would soon benefit from the music.

CHAPTER 4 – 1986
THE MUSIC WORLD IS BREAKING UP:
GENRE-BENDING IS BREAKING THE GROUND FOR GRUNGE

"WHAT HAPPENED, ROB? DID YOU FALL ASLEEP UNDER A CAR AND HAVE OIL DRIP ON YOUR head?" said my friend and classmate, Franco referring to the amount of gel I would have in my hair every day. What can I say, I had a thick head of black hair that would stand up and just be wild without gel or mousse, so I slathered that stuff on as if my life depended on it. This would become an almost daily question, and I'd have some stupid quip shot back at Franco, but he always won because, well, sometimes it did look like I had oil in my hair.

Franco and I connected over more than insults and jabs, we connected over music. I was a rock guy, a metalhead, and he was a rap fan. He was also one of the few black kids in my school and in the mid-'80s in Brooklyn, not everyone in our predominantly white neighborhood was comfortable with white kids being friends with black kids. This was mainly a concern of racist white adults, not the kids in our school. No one cared what color or nationality anyone was. All we cared about was if you were good at sports and did you like cool music. And Franco liked cool music.

1986 was the perfect year for him and me to discuss music because it was the year that Aerosmith and Run-D.M.C. released their massive collaboration of the song "Walk This Way," originally released by Aerosmith in 1975. '86 also saw the release of Licensed To Ill by three white rappers from New York called, Beastie Boys. Franco and I were in our glory. I was able to turn him onto rock music a bit more than he was, and as I was discovering rap, he helped me find the best of what was out there. This was true collaboration . . . and friendship!

I spent many 1986 spring and summer nights in my room, fingers lined up with the "record & play" buttons on my boombox, and the radio tuned to WBLS's "Rap Attack" with Mr. Magic and Marley Marl. I was thirteen years old and couldn't afford to buy albums very often so the only way to listen to the songs I loved whenever I wanted to was to wait for them to come on the radio. You can't imagine how angry I'd get at myself if I missed the songs I was waiting for. Turns out I had the patience to wait for what I wanted and good enough timing to not miss the songs once the DJs played them.

Rap came into my consciousness in the mid-'80s, particularly, in 1986. Two albums piqued my interest in this new sound hailing from the Bronx, NY. Both records were made by artists from Queens, New York but it is largely agreed upon that the birthplace of rap music is the Bronx. I had been devouring *King of Rock* and *Radio* by Run-DMC and LL Cool J respectively. I was a bona fide fan of this new musical style and was actively looking for more of it. I didn't have to wait long as albums by Whodini, Doug E. Fresh and the Get Fresh Crew, Beastie Boys, and another album by Run-DMC would all drop in '86. I recorded songs by these artists and many others throughout the year, making mixtapes for myself and anyone else who cared to listen.

Only a few of my friends at the time, maybe three or four, were really into rap music that early on. That was fine though because I was still very much into heavy metal, and hard rock, and had begun listening to punk as well, so I had plenty of people that I could still discuss music with. Besides, rap was so new and so different, it was almost better that I had just a small group of friends to share it with. It felt like we had stumbled upon something so raw

CHAPTER 4 – 1986: THE MUSIC WORLD IS BREAKING UP

and dangerous that it wasn't meant to be shared with everyone. We were already hearing that rap, "wasn't music" and it was, "just a fad" from adults and closed-minded people who couldn't accept anything new regarding popular music. This made being a rap fan feel cooler. In a way, it was like what being a fan of punk rock was. It was music for the outcasts and the underground. It wasn't for society at large. It was for the people on the street, in the clubs, and anywhere else where change was exciting and necessary. People whom the mainstream was afraid of and didn't understand like DJs, B-Boys, MCs, breakdancers, and graffiti artists were at the forefront of bringing rap music to the masses.

Listening to rap back then was like getting a front-row seat in a world many people, namely white people, didn't know (or want to know for that matter) existed. So, the short-sighted take that rap wasn't music and just a fad would soon change as it wouldn't be long before the world caught on and accepted this new and exciting musical genre. Rap was yet another step toward the seismic shift in music and culture that was just a few years away in the early 1990s and those of us who were along for the start of this ride felt it coming.

On May 15, 1986 (my thirteenth birthday), Run-DMC released an album that would change music. I say that because it was the album that just about every rapper from that era would point to as the reason, they wanted to start making their own rap records. *Raising Hell*, released on Profile Records, is arguably the most important rap album of all time. Everything in music must be discussed in the context of era and influence. Have there been hip-hop albums that have sold more copies? Of course. Can one argue that other rap albums are better (as subjective as that is) than *Raising Hell*? Absolutely. However, at the time of its release, just as rap was starting to gain some momentum and was trying desperately to fight off the powers that be in the mainstream music industry and a large percentage of the American population as well, *Raising Hell* not only won the fight, but it also created an army of confident and loyal followers who became huge rap stars as well. These artists would become the first wave of a new genre that would one day be known as one of the biggest musical genres on the planet. Raising Hell changed the rap game forever. I would even say that it was to Run-DMC what *Sgt. Pepper's* was to The Beatles. Both albums, in the era and culture they were released in, drew clear lines in the sand and created a "before and after" conversation surrounding the respective records.

Helping matters in making rap music a genre that was here to stay was the suggestion by one of the album's co-producers, a fledgling music executive/DJ named Rick Rubin, to cover a song by hard rock legends Aerosmith called "Walk This Way." The song, a top ten hit for Aerosmith when it was first released in 1975, "Walk This Way" was frequently used by deejays as a breakbeat favorite in the era before rap records even existed. Rubin, whose favorite band as a teenager was Aerosmith, not only suggested recording the song but invited Steven Tyler and Joe Perry, the band's lead singer and lead guitarist, respectively, to join Run-DMC on the new recording. Add a hit music video to the mix and the remake of "Walk This Way" became one of the biggest songs released at that time. It turns out, it was also one of the biggest songs ever to be released.

Let's not forget too that black music in America hadn't had an easy road to the top. For instance, many people credit Elvis Presley with creating rock 'n' roll , he's even nicknamed "The King," but it was black blues music that Elvis was performing. A lyric from the legendary 1989 song, "Fight The Power" by one of hip-hop's originators, Public Enemy states the distaste for Elvis as a "straight up racist" and to "mother fuck him and John Wayne."

Elvis would always vehemently deny being a racist and would give props to the black musicians his music came from. In a 1957 interview with JET Magazine, Elvis said, "A lot of people seemed to think I started this business, but rock 'n' roll was here a long time before I came along. Nobody can sing

CHAPTER 4 - 1986: THE MUSIC WORLD IS BREAKING UP

that music like colored people. I can't sing like Fats Domino can. I know that."

Chuck D of Public Enemy has gotten flack for the lyric I referred to in "Fight The Power," and he would explain his stance on Elvis and the meaning behind the lyric over time. In 2002, Chuck would tell the New York newspaper, *Newsday*, "My whole thing was the one-sidedness. Elvis' icon status in America made it like nobody else counted. My heroes came from someone else. My heroes came before him. My heroes were probably his heroes. As far as Elvis being the king, I couldn't buy that."

You'd have to be naive to think that race didn't play a role in the initial backlash against this new, black, urban music. Combining a classic and beloved hard rock band like Aerosmith with three young black men who were the face of a new style of music eased tensions enough to give rap a chance. What they did with that chance was change the world.

There are a few moments in one's lifetime that cannot be erased. Age is a major factor of course because something that happened when you were two years old would likely not be remembered, no matter how important or even catastrophic the moment was. By the time you're a teenager though, you are very likely to remember events that are large in scope. Late morning, January 28, 1986, was one such moment. At 11:39 AM EST, the Space Shuttle Challenger exploded seventy-three seconds after its launch from Cape Canaveral, Florida. If ever time stood still, the seconds and minutes after this tragedy took place, time certainly stood still. Watching the horror unfold with my classmates at school, was the single most shocking thing I had witnessed in my young life at that point. How could something like this happen? The lead-up to the voyage was everywhere since one of the crew members, Christa McAuliffe, was going to be the first schoolteacher in space. The media coverage of her appointment to the Challenger team had captivated the country and the world. And in a flash, she, and the other six astronauts on board were killed, live on television.

A country left mourning the Challenger disaster would soon be angered by foul play in the highest ranks of its government. In November of '86, a report that the United States had been selling weapons to Iran in secret, to secure the release of seven American hostages being held by pro-Iranian groups in Lebanon. This was a major discovery in the ongoing Iran-Contra affair, during the Reagan administration that had begun as far back as 1981 when senior administration officials secretly facilitated the sale of arms to Iran which was the subject of an arms embargo at the time. The administration hoped to use the proceeds of the arms sale to fund the Contras, a right-wing rebel group, in Nicaragua. Further complicating matters was the shredding of documents by National Security Council member Oliver North and his secretary, Fawn Hall, implicating them in selling weapons to Iran and channeling the proceeds to help fund the Contra rebels in Nicaragua.

The combination of sadness from the Challenger explosion and the anger toward the U.S. government brought on by its behavior during the Iran-Contra affair was just the type of cultural event that would lead the youth of America to display their feelings in new and loud ways. Although its roots can be traced back to the '70s, the hardcore punk scene, mainly emanating from New York City's Lower East Side, flourished in the early and mid-'80s, with a lot of its inherent aggression aimed at political and societal institutions. Hardcore being younger, faster, and angrier than traditional punk rock, took its attitude from adolescents who were sick of their life in a "bland Republican America" as some on the scene would put it. Hardcore punk lyrics often express anti-authoritarian, anti-establishment, anti-violence, and pro-environmentalist sentiments. During the 1980s the hardcore scene often rejected what was perceived to be yuppie materialism and interventionist American foreign policy. Numerous hardcore punk bands expressed opposition to political leaders such as Ronald Reagan and British Prime Minister Margaret Thatcher. Reagan's economic policies, referred to by some as Reaganomics,

CHAPTER 4 - 1986: THE MUSIC WORLD IS BREAKING UP

and social conservatism were common subjects for criticism by hardcore bands of the time.

Speaking of Manhattan's Lower East Side, the end of the year would be witness to the second rap phenomenon which would take what Run-DMC did and catapult the genre into the stratosphere for good. Not only would rap music never be the same but alternative rock, both sonically and as a scene, still a few years away from the limelight, would get one of its biggest and most important ambassadors in New York City's Beastie Boys.

Formed from the ashes of the experimental hardcore punk band, The Young Aborigines, the Beastie Boys would originate in 1981. After a few lineup changes, former Young Aborigines vocalist Michael Diamond (Mike D), along with Adam Yauch (MCA), and Adam Horovitz (Ad-Rock) would comprise the new group. Continuing as a hardcore punk band, the Beastie Boys would slowly incorporate the new sounds of rap they were hearing on the New York City streets where they came from, into their musical repertoire. On November 15, 1986, the band released its debut album via Def Jam and Columbia Records, *Licensed to Ill*.

Licensed to Ill became the first rap album to reach #1 on the Billboard album chart. It is one of Columbia Records' fastest-selling debut records and received critical acclaim for its unique musical style, chemistry between the group members, and their inventive, stylized vocal chops. Since its release, *Licensed to Ill* has been ranked by critics as one of the greatest hip-hop and debut albums of all time.

On the heels of Run-DMC and Aerosmith's crossover smash hit, "Walk This Way," creating a path for rap to infiltrate white America, now you had three white guys incorporating heavy metal guitar riffs and huge rock drumbeats sampled from Led Zeppelin, and it suddenly wasn't so far-fetched to see why rap was gaining steam. Although the lyrics on *Licensed to Ill* were largely sophomoric, the Beasties were catering to the frat boy, middle-America types for acceptance and record sales. It was difficult to tell at the time if the band was for real or an odd parody of the new genre. No one had seen anyone quite like them before and even with their less-than-serious antics and lyrical content, there was an obvious charm and talent that the Beastie Boys had. This led to respect from those already in the rap community like Run-DMC and LL Cool J. The trio would even get airplay on the various rap radio shows. Back then there weren't any rap radio stations, but most R&B stations would play rap at night and the Beastie Boys were included on most playlists. Years later, after another album or two, the Beastie Boys would shed the frat boy/wild jock image, and truly take their place amongst the greatest rappers of all time.

As the Seattle scene was steadily building steam in 1986, the upstart rap scene, which now had ascended to the top of the charts, was created in and flourished through, a geographical music scene in the inner cities of New York. Word of mouth, local, regional, national, and international shows and tours, radio and MTV airplay, conventional advertising, and the major record labels all had a hand in creating scenes and even deciding which ones would find success and which ones would die before they had a chance at fame and fortune. Living in my Brooklyn, NY bubble, I was lucky enough that NYC, along with L.A., was the epicenter of the entertainment world. If something was happening in music, I'd likely know about it long before people who didn't live in an entertainment mecca. Hip-hop was a uniquely American art form, as the Blues was decades before, but quickly found itself traversing the globe and influencing people in places you wouldn't think possible.

When I spoke with renowned hip-hop producer and PhD, Configa (whose real name is Andrew Laidlaw, Arrested Development, Chuck D, etc.), I was intrigued by what turned him onto hip-hop considering he was born and raised in England, and as is often the case with American music and culture, rap didn't make its way across the Atlantic in a major way until around 1988.

"Run-DMC was the first hip-hop artist I had heard of. They were the

CHAPTER 4 - 1986: THE MUSIC WORLD IS BREAKING UP

trailblazers as far as I was concerned. LL Cool J as well. Both, along with a few other acts had set the tone for what was to come in the '90s here in England," said Configa as we discussed where his love and desire for this new phenomenon called rap music came from. Like so many other artists I've spoken with, Configa simply knew this music was going to somehow play a role in the rest of his life. He told me about the exact moment when this happened to him.

"I was listening to the radio one day and the normal, boring crap was being played, and suddenly this song, 'Potholes in My Lawn' by De La Soul, (the band's second single off their album *3 Feet High and Rising*) came on and I was like, 'What the fuck is this?' It was like BAM, it just hit me. It felt like the soundtrack to the promised land. I made sure to remember the name and I went to HMV to try and find it. I was asking them, have you got De La Soul? No? Oh, it's over there, ok. No one really knew. I eventually found it and started my research right then and there. No internet yet, no MTV Raps. It was a voyage of discovery and what a beautiful one at that. A few short years later, it all just got massive. Ice Cube, Dre with *The Chronic*, Tupac, Biggie was on the scene not too long after, Nas, Wu-Tang, it just exploded."

Hip-Hop, or Rap as it was commonly referred to in the '80s, wasn't the only music that influenced Configa. Of course, he cites bands and artists such as Public Enemy, Arrested Development, Ice Cube, Dr. Dre, and others as his major influences, but growing up in England with parents who liked many types of music, Configa had a taste for it all.

"I liked rock music, and still do," he said. "At the time that I was discovering rap music, a band like Living Colour caught my attention as I hadn't seen black guys playing hard rock. It was so authentic."

What makes a statement like that even more interesting is that Configa is white. Not only did he grow up half a world away from where Hip-Hop was born, but because he was white, at least back in the '80s and early '90s, this new genre was being branded as "black music" and nothing more than a fad. I remember the attitudes and racial discussions during the '80s as well and thankfully the people who deemed rap as a fad or even worse, not music at all, have been proven wrong a million times over. It's woven throughout the book how music touches some people in ways that are difficult to fully explain. It has the power to create new cultures and shift existing ones for the better. Race, religion, geography, and social and economic status meant nothing to those in the underground of the late '80s leading into 1990 and beyond, and Configa's success is more proof of this.

Speaking with Configa, strangely, is like speaking with myself at times. This is the connection music can make. I mentioned earlier that he has a PhD, and he did so by writing his thesis on the intersection of Hip-Hop culture and ethnicity, exploring the music scene in England. I do not have a PhD but I did write this book on the music and culture that I love, and what it's done for multiple generations, so it's not a stretch to say that Configa and I are cut from the same musical cloth as it concerns who we are at our core.

When Configa speaks about the days when Hip-Hop first shook his world and how relevant it is in his life today, he has this to say, "The golden era of Hip-Hop is still out there today. Many artists still use it as inspiration. I do as well. I'll go back to the classics, it gets me going, man! A night out, as just a vibe to chill, I go back to it all the time."

Back in the Pacific Northwest, the underground music scene was inching slowly toward the mainstream surface. Sub Pop, founded by Bruce Pavitt and Jonathan Poneman in 1986, as an offshoot of Pavitt's fanzine, Subterranean Pop which got its start in the early '80s, was looking to highlight underground and alternative music both nationally and internationally in the mid and late '80s. Although Sub Pop's first release was a compilation made up of bands that weren't from Seattle, (the first Sub Pop LP was the compilation Sub Pop 100, featuring songs by artists including Sonic Youth, Naked Raygun, Wipers, and Scratch Acid) the label's decision to work on Green River's *Dry as a Bone*, helped the new label gain a foothold in Seattle where in a few short years they would gain success and notoriety around the globe. The sig-

CHAPTER 4 - 1986: THE MUSIC WORLD IS BREAKING UP

nificance of this record would be two-fold. First, the sound picked up where their previous release left off, but the band had now perfected its sludgy, fuzzy persona which would kick off the grunge movement. Green River was tighter as a band at this point as their playing had drastically improved from the *Come On Down* days. Second, and probably the most important aspect of this release, the band chose to work with Pavitt and Poneman, helping to solidify an already tight-knit local music community.

As is common with most new, independent record labels, Sub Pop didn't have the funds to release *Dry as a Bone* upon its completion in 1986, so a year later, as was the case with *Come On Down, Dry as a Bone* saw the light of day. Promoted by Sub Pop as "ultra-loose grunge that destroyed the morals of a generation" (Michael Azzerad's Our Band Could Be Your Life), giving birth to not just the latest release by Green River, but also, according to many, the first time the word "grunge" was used to describe the sound of a band from the Seattle area. As they say, the rest is history.

CHAPTER 5 – 1987
GRUNGE SPROUT ROOTS: WHEN THE TERM GRUNGE STARTED ITS JOURNEY TOWARD COMMERCIALIZATION

"I'VE HAD IT UP TO HERE WITH YOUR SHIT!" THIS WAS THE FIRST AND ONLY TIME I'VE EVER heard my mother curse, and it was jarring. I was fourteen years old and lingering in the kitchen with the refrigerator door wide open. It's a strange thing we do with the fridge, isn't it? I know it's not just me. Admit it, you stand there, peering into this cold box that keeps you fed as if you're looking for the missing link. In my house in the '80s, it was highly unlikely that the contents within would be any different than the usual eight to ten staples I always saw. Yet still, I stood there looking into the bright light and cold air searching for the meaning of life. Spoiler alert, I didn't find it.

Hearing a parent curse for the first time is surprising and unsettling. It makes them . . . human. Sometimes children look at their parents as creatures without a discovered species. They're just these beings that run your life and take care of you for a time but for some reason, especially in your teenage years, you're continuously looking to escape their reign. I loved my mother, and I still do. But I was a lost and angry young man, going through some very difficult emotions at the time so my behavior and utter indifference to her feelings that day in the kitchen did illicit and warrant my mother's reaction to me.

Brooklyn was all I knew. School, sports, and friends were all just blocks from each other. I didn't want to leave. My mother was currently engaged to a very nice man, her long-term boyfriend, and the plan was for them to marry and move the family to Staten Island. If you're not familiar with New York, the city is made up of five boroughs: Brooklyn, Queens, Manhattan, the Bronx, and Staten Island. The last on the list was separated from the others by the Verrazzano-Narrows bridge. At that point in my life, it may as well have been separated by the entire Atlantic Ocean because if we moved to Staten Island, I knew I'd rarely, if ever, see my friends again. The prospect of moving there gave me all the ammunition I needed to treat my mother and her fiancé like trash. They never got married.

If we agree that 1991 was the year a new genre exploded into the mainstream, and 1984 was when the fuse was lit, then I'd make the argument that 1987 was the year that the spark on that fuse had passed the point of no return and never to be doused. Hindsight is a wonderful thing because it's easier to look back now and see there was something brewing, something just off the horizon that was patiently waiting to wreak havoc over the safe and bland youth culture. I'd be lying if I said I knew what was coming back then, I didn't. All I knew was that the music I was listening to be it rap, metal, hard rock, punk, or alternative/college, was filling me up with feelings and emotions that excited me. I was ready for the change ahead, even if I didn't know a change was coming.

The first brick to fall in the emergence of hard, loud rock taking over the mainstream happened in the summer of 1987 with the release of Guns N' Roses debut album, *Appetite for Destruction*. Seemingly coming out of nowhere, the L.A. band was gaining momentum since its debut was released and made it to the top of the US Billboard 200 chart as well as the Top Hard Rock Albums chart by the end of the year. The band, and the album,

CHAPTER 5 - 1987: GRUNGE SPROUT ROOTS

were fierce, unpredictable, and without knowing it, setting the world up for various forms of hard rock music to soon dominate the television and radio airwaves. This may have only been the beginning, but the transformation was officially underway. We were still using monikers, hard rock, and heavy metal to describe heavy, loud, fast, rock 'n' roll , but a new name was bubbling just beneath the surface.

What made the grunge era different from other large musical genres is that contrary to popular belief, grunge wasn't a sound as much as it was a scene and a mindset. It's usually helpful (but sometimes lazy) to name musical genres so we all know what to reference when we want to discuss certain styles of music. Every genre has sub-genres that flow into and out of the main genre, but for the most part, the sound of the music is what's being described.

We all know hip-hop when we hear it. With its infectious beats and rhythmic lyrical flow, although it has so many sub-genres attached, there's no mistaking it's hip-hop. The same can be said for the twang of country, the snarl of punk rock, the danceability of disco, the bludgeoning speed of heavy metal, the soothing sounds of Motown, the complex intricacies of jazz, and so on. There will be outliers in every era and genre, but for the most part, the sounds of these genres are relatively easy to identify.

Grunge is a bit different. If there is a sound that's attached to the name it's essentially heavy metal, '70s hard rock, and punk, mixed with personal and introspective lyrics. The problem is many of the bands that are associated with grunge don't sound that much alike. Due to Nirvana's meteoric ascension in 1991 and 1992, the media and record companies, as well as corporate America, needed to call it something. But as we're still in 1987, and the word they would eventually nominate as "the term" for the new music Nirvana was championing in the early '90s, would just start to see the light of day. The powers that be started digging into a few interviews from some of the early Seattle movers and shakers like Mark Arm of Green River and Mudhoney,

Buzz Osbourne of the Melvins, and Bruce Pavitt of Sub Pop Records and they would find their marketing version of gold.

Stumbling upon the term "grunge" from a letter written to the fanzine *Desperate Times* by none other than Mark Arm, describing the sound of his first band in the early '80s, Mr. Epp and the Calculations as "Pure noise, pure grunge, pure shit!" could have been where they lifted the term from. Or, it could quite possibly have come from a quote attributed to Sub-Pop cofounder, Bruce Pavitt when he said, "gritty vocals, roaring Marshall amps, ultra-loose grunge that destroyed the morals of a generation" when talking about the EP, *Dry as a Bone* by Green River in 1987.

And voila, a name that would become a price tag was born.

Marketers and advertisers must come up with words or catchphrases that will stick to society's ears long enough to profit from them. If some of the original folks on the scene used the term "grunge" to describe this new music, and no one had come up with anything better, it made sense to use the artist's terminology to sell the scene. So, when people came across Mark Arm's quote in the fanzine *Desperate Times* describing the music of his first band Mr. Epp and the Calculations as "pure shit, pure noise, pure grunge," a genre was born.

It's understandable if you think of it from a marketing perspective, and isn't that what most of the music business is all about anyway? Nirvana, along with the rest of the early grunge bands, were from the Pacific Northwest where in many places, namely Seattle, it tends to be gray, rainy, misty, and dark . . . grungy if you will. The script wrote itself. Outside of the almighty dollar though, if the powers that be had listened to the music for the music's sake, they would've realized that in addition to the hard rock/metal/punk fusion that came together to give grunge its first blueprint, there was another huge influence on the sound and that was the music of the alternative underground and American college scene.

1987 was a very important year as massively influential releases such as *The Joshua Tree* (U2), *Document* (R.E.M.), *Kiss Me, Kiss Me, Kiss Me* (The

CHAPTER 5 - 1987: GRUNGE SPROUT ROOTS

Cure), *Pleased to Meet Me* (The Replacements), *Kick* (INXS), and *Jane's Addiction* (Jane's Addiction) paved the way for other artists to follow in their footsteps but also for fans and commercial radio/tv to start getting accustomed to a new, faster, and heavier sound. Grunge, as it's been stated, has many sounds and styles built into it. Some may think it's all doom and gloom with distorted guitars, but that assertion would be incorrect. Nirvana, for example, borrowed the jangly guitar sound of R.E.M. and Sonic Youth and some of the pop sensibilities of The Cure. The rawness of The Replacements could be found in some of the harder songs by Pearl Jam, specifically off their albums, *Vs.* and *Vitalogy*. Examples like these can be found throughout the rise of grunge.

In addition to the bands and records above, some other big names released albums in 1987 which only heightened the still burgeoning scene. Bands like Depeche Mode, Husker Du, Sonic Youth, Faith No More, The Smiths, Public Enemy, Siouxse & the Banshees, and the Red Hot Chili Peppers all put out records that would influence countless artists a few short years later. The emergence of alternative and college rock, combined with what was happening in and around Seattle in the mid-'80s, were the ingredients that would soon inform the new rock sound known as grunge. With so many diverse and unique bands creating this blend, it's no wonder that anyone who got branded with the "grunge" tag wasn't all that happy about it.

With all these influences to draw from, and despite superficial labels and titles, bands like Nirvana and others from the Pacific Northwest would start to build up a head of steam and creep their way toward superstardom.

I mentioned earlier (Chapter 2, 1984) that we hadn't heard the last of Green River and that's because the band's collective fingerprints are permanently smeared all over the grunge and alternative movement. With in-fighting based on disagreements surrounding musical direction at an all-time high in the middle of 1987, the band essentially ceased to exist by October of that year. The band was still in the middle of working on what would become its final album, *Rehab Doll*, and agreed to finish the project before completely parting ways although its members would immediately start new bands while putting the finishing touches on the record. Rehab Doll was eventually released in June 1988.

After playing in a cover band with some friends before figuring out exactly what they wanted to do, Mother Love Bone was formed in 1987 by Jeff Ament, Bruce Fairweather, and Stone Gossard (ex-Green River members), ex-Malfunkshun frontman Andrew Wood, and Greg Gilmore, formerly of Ten Minute Warning.

The new band began recording music and playing shows almost immediately and by late 1988 had become one of Seattle's more promising bands. Lead singer Andrew Wood's flamboyant on-stage personality, look, and introspective lyrics helped bring music industry-wide attention to the band. Although interest in the band was high, the lifespan of Mother Love Bone wasn't destined to last very long. Like Green River before them, however, this is not the last we'll hear from the short-lived band as its influence has lasted 30-plus years and counting.

Formed in Aberdeen, Washington, Nirvana was the brainchild of singer/guitarist Kurt Cobain and bassist Krist Novoselic. The two aspiring musicians, influenced by '60s and '70s rock, along with the punk and underground scene emanating from their home state and beyond, met in high school while frequenting practices from local heroes, the Melvins. The band's first album wouldn't be released until 1989, but Nirvana would be a factor within the Seattle music scene soon after they'd get together. They would release their first single in late 1988, a cover of Shocking Blue's "Love Buzz" on Sub Pop Records but their biggest impact on the indie scene would come in mid-1989 with their debut album, *Bleach*. More about Nirvana in the coming chapters but the fact that the band got its start in 1987 just adds to the importance of this breakthrough year.

Just as the tides were slowly changing within music, I was also changing.

CHAPTER 5 - 1987: GRUNGE SPROUT ROOTS

In 1987 I was in the eighth grade and getting ready for high school. That's an interesting and often stressful time in the life of a teenager. I was starting to look at life a little differently as graduating from grammar school is a bit of a milestone in a young person's life. It's an uncertain, yet exciting time and I was looking forward to the change. One such change was the prospect of leaving my childhood home (and city for that matter) and moving to a new place, schools I wasn't familiar with, and new kids. This was happening because my mom was engaged to be married to her long-time boyfriend, and we were about to move in with him and his two daughters from his first marriage. I wasn't interested in leaving my friends, my house, or my neighborhood as they were all I'd known up until this point in my life.

Being fourteen is tough enough but being fourteen, growing up in a divorced household, and trying to process your mom getting married to a new man all while leaving everything you know makes things incredibly tough. Psychologically and emotionally, I wasn't ready. This was evident in my behavior toward my mother, her soon-to-be husband, and anyone else I felt like pissing off. I was a jerk.

I remember one instance when I was in the King's Plaza Mall on Flatbush Avenue and Avenue U in Brooklyn, and my mom was so angry with me because of my unrelenting poor attitude and defiant behavior, that she screamed at me on a crowded escalator and my initial reaction was to jump off and run away. Now, I didn't think far enough ahead to realize that had I jumped I'd likely break a leg (or worse) and wouldn't be running anywhere. Just that thought running through my head showed how angry, conflicted, and confused I was back then and that I'd risk severe personal injury to escape. I'll admit that I wasn't a pleasure to be around during those days but being young and confused about who I was and what my parents even meant to me certainly played a role in creating my less-than-appropriate behavior.

As it turns out, I never did move as my mom broke off the engagement (for reasons I'm still unsure of) and I didn't have to face the prospects of navigating all that change. Although I was quite relieved, I still went through all the emotions leading up to this last-minute decision and I know it left me scarred. Music was what I'd always turn to when things took a left turn in my life and this time was no exception. I was very much into rap, punk, and what I referred to as college music (soon to be known globally as alternative), and my passion for it all was growing by the day. Some of the albums I used to blur the lines of reality with were *Introduce Yourself* by Faith No More, *Document*, R.E.M., *Kick* by INXS, *Pleased to Meet Me*, The Replacements, Prince's *Sign O' The Times*, *Appetite for Destruction* by Guns N' Roses, *Paid in Full*, Erik B. and Rakim, *Criminal Minded* by Boogie Down Productions, *Bigger and Deffer*, LL Cool J, *Yo! Bum Rush the Show* by Public Enemy, and others spoke to me in a way other music didn't. These records, although different in sound and style, all had one thing in common, at least I felt they did. They seemed to take desperation and angst and turn them into a drive and a future destination. They felt raw and emotional and that's exactly what I was feeling.

Still unable to reconcile my parents' divorce and growing up without my dad as a daily figure in my life, pondering life with an adopted family by way of my mother's pending wedding, then when that didn't happen, being stuck in the same confusion as before with no guide, except the music, to show me a positive way out.

In line with the feelings of desperation and depression I was feeling back then, looking at it now, almost forty years later, it's no wonder why the music I was falling in love with at the time was so important to me. I assumed then, and know now, that I was not alone. The late '80s/early '90s was the incubation period for myself and others like me, which spawned a lifelong love and appreciation of the music and the developing scene that we'd carry into adulthood and eventually, our livelihoods.

"Music saved my life on numerous occasions," said John Richards, longtime host and producer of The Morning Show on Seattle's 90.3 KEXP-FM, one of the area's most popular and influential radio stations dating back to

CHAPTER 5 - 1987: GRUNGE SPROUT ROOTS

1972. John's show has been responsible for breaking bands like The Lumineers, The National, and many others as well as being the on-air leader in fundraising over the years on KEXP. He also heads up several shows and causes on air reminding his listeners "You are not alone."

John has been a fixture on the Seattle music scene since the early '90s and when he and I spoke for the book, I learned that I had a kindred spirit in Seattle while I was experiencing similar things to him at the start of the grunge and alternative movement.

"I was fourteen or fifteen years old," John said. "Going through a really tough spot with depression and eventually dropped out of high school during my freshman year. I really hit rock bottom."

It was around this time that John's older brother (five years his senior) had started sharing music with him that in John's words, "Turned out to be the weirdest, most insane sounds I'd ever heard up until that point in my life. It turned out to be 'Come on Pilgrim' by the Pixies off Surfer Rosa. If this existed, what else was out there?"

We've certainly heard the Pixies mentioned numerous times already in the book (and more to come) so it's clear that kids everywhere were starting to discover them early enough to lead them to the eventual music promise land that was early '90s Seattle.

"After a while," John said about hearing the Pixies, "without really knowing it, I was waking up every morning looking forward to the day thinking what am I going to listen to today?"

I can easily relate to this behavior because I did the exact same thing. I'd hear a new song, by some band I didn't know, lose my mind over it, and look for the next one. This only intensified for me, (as for John) once live music entered our world.

Talking about the first band Richards saw live, Jane's Addiction, he'd say, "When Perry (Farrell) screams, 'Comin down the mountain' (a lyric from the band's track 'Mountain Song') . . . whatever the fuck that is, I want to do every day for the rest of my life."

John may have been in Seattle, and I was almost 3,000 miles away in New York, but we were experiencing the same things with our minds, hearts, and ears. The difference was that was in the epicenter of it all and I was watching from afar. He's gone on to know and befriend many of the scene's biggest stars and yet he's humbled and gracious. Hell, if I've eaten dinner at Jeff Ament's house (bassist and co-founder of Green River, Mother Love Bone, and Pearl Jam), I'm not so sure how humble I'd be.

"I didn't know it at the time," Richards continues, "but I was geographically in the right location at the right time, and at the right age where I didn't have a care in the world and music became everything."

We went on to discuss not only the timing and the location of where he came of age but also the power that music has to heal. John Richards is a selfless mental health advocate as he's struggled with his own mental health throughout his life. He knows he has a platform, and he takes that seriously and without compromise.

"I owe music everything," he said. "And if I can help at least one person from hurting themselves or giving up on themselves, and I can do that through music, that's what I'm going to do. We were in the middle of one of the greatest musical movements in history and it saved me. The music being made in Seattle back then was so relatable, you felt like you knew the people making it. That music shaped who I am. There's no doubt about it in my mind."

As busy as he is on air, John's responsibilities off-air include managing the on-air sound through his management of over 40 DJs while simultaneously creating various specialty shows. John is also responsible for the Music Heals series which works at the intersection of music and mental health. John Richards hosts events and works on music supervision for movies, television, and businesses. John also owns and runs Life on Mars, a plant-based bar located in the center of Capital Hill in Seattle, which also includes a vinyl record shop

CHAPTER 5 - 1987: GRUNGE SPROUT ROOTS

inside. His most important work is raising two boys and being married to his wife Amy, with whom he cohosts The Dr. and the DJ Podcast about music, health, and life.

Culturally, two events occurred that would, like grunge and alternative music, begin quietly enough in the late 1980s but be a harbinger of what was to come in the next decade and help define that, and many decades to follow. "The Simpsons," a new cartoon short created by Matt Groening and produced by James L. Brooks is shown for the first time on The Tracey Ullman Show, April 19, 1987. The premise focused on the antics of the dysfunctional Simpsons family of Homer, Marge, Bart, Lisa, and Maggie and was loosely based on Groening's own family.

The series aired on the newly launched Fox television network and a total of 48 Simpsons shorts were shown before they were turned into their own series in 1989. The cartoon would go on to become one of the most successful, long-lasting, and influential shows in the history of television. As a fourteen-year-old in 1987, the smart comedy, edgy content, and what seemed like a big middle finger to typical American sitcoms at the time, the show caught my attention and just like the underground music I was discovering at that same time, felt like it was being created for me.

Another monumental event, this time of the negative persuasion, happened on October 19, 1987. That date, known as "Black Monday," was at the time, the largest ever one-day stock market loss. As recent rapid growth in the United States had started to slow in the Fall of 1987, the Dow Jones Industrial Index reflected declining optimism after its August peak. Global stock markets were already showing signs of nervousness when Hong Kong's Seng Index crashed which had ripple effects throughout Europe. Soon after, U.S. warships attacked Iranian oil platforms in response to missile attacks on an American ship, and Wall St. felt the shrapnel. The collective meltdown destroyed nearly half the world's paper wealth as the Dow Jones fell 508 points losing over $500 billion.

I'm not going to pretend this affected me in 1987 nor am I going to pretend that I could intelligently explain what the stock market was back then. Hell, I can barely explain it now. What I will say though is that this crash was colossal news and every adult within earshot of me was panicked. Not the greatest scenario for an already fragile kid, with no money to begin with, to be spending his time worrying about. It was just another log on the fire of anger, confusion, boredom, resentment, and isolation that I was feeling and as it turned out, many young songwriters were as well.

CHAPTER 6 – 1988-1990
IT'S ALWAYS DARKEST BEFORE THE DAWN: A SOCIETY IN TURMOIL AND THE MUSIC TO FOLLOW

"WHY WOULD THEY MAKE FUN OF YOU, THEY'RE YOUR FRIENDS?" ASKED ONE OF MY HIGH school teachers I confided in about writing poetry. "There's absolutely nothing wrong with poetry or writing in general, you know that," he continued. As I thought for a moment, I knew he was right regarding poetry or any form of writing, but he may have been too far removed from adolescence to remember the pitfalls of admitting things to your friends that were outside the norm. In this case, I assumed writing poetry was way outside the norm that I'd dare never to share this information.

"I don't know, maybe you're right, never mind. I appreciate you listening to me," and with that, I didn't speak to anyone about my poetry for probably the next two decades. Looking back on that decision to keep my writing to myself wasn't the worst idea. Not because I was all that concerned about my friends (many from grammar and high school I still have today) shunning me. They wouldn't have, they're great guys and I love them. The problem was my self-esteem was quite low, therapy hadn't helped much to this point (even though I'd go back soon enough), and showing my creative side to anyone, even my closest friends, was just something you didn't do in Brooklyn during the 1980s. Besides, my poems were mostly autobiographical, and they contained dark, sad themes that I wasn't ready to share with anyone. Reading them again while doing research for this book, I was not only depressed back then, I subtly flirted with thoughts of suicide.

It cannot be said enough that 1991, musically speaking, didn't just simply fall out of the sky. As noted in the previous chapter, Nirvana began its career in 1987 and all the seedlings that turned into the grunge movement had been sewn as early as 1984. The underground garage rock of the 1960s laid the earliest seeds, but for more contemporary bands, the early '80s marked the beginnings of what would happen globally starting in 1991. Unbeknownst to the rest of the planet, 1988-1990 would prove to be the final ramp-up, both musically and culturally, for the groundbreaking events just on the horizon.

Soundgarden, one of the biggest and most important bands of the 1990s (and beyond), as far as the grunge and alternative movement was concerned, released its debut album in '88 and set the tone for how the world would soon look to Seattle as its musical compass. *Ultramega ok* was released on October 31, 1988, via SST Records. The band had already been gaining local notoriety for its EPs *Screaming Life* and *Fopp*, both on Seattle's Sub Pop Records before its debut LP. *Ultramega ok* is a disjointed effort in terms of style and sound but there were glimpses on that record as to what this band had the potential to become. Not surprisingly, the spotlight was on lead singer/guitarist and main songwriter, Chris Cornell. Years later, Cornell would be recognized as one of the greatest rock singers and songwriters in rock music, but in 1988, he was just starting to assert his future dominance.

1988 saw yet another remnant of grunge rock's "patient zero," Green River, emerge with the formation of Mudhoney. As was the case of former Green River alum, Jeff Ament, Stone Gossard, and Bruce Fairweather before them, Mark Arm, and Steve Turner would create a band of their own in January of '88. Turner and Arm began writing songs with Bundle of Hiss

CHAPTER 6 - 1988-1990: IT'S ALWAYS DARKEST BEFORE THE DAWN

drummer Dan Peters and eventually recruited former Melvins bassist Matt Lukin to round out the new outfit.

The four-piece released its debut EP, *Superfuzz Bigmuff* on Sub Pop in October of the same year. The record's first single, "Touch Me I'm Sick" helped the band attain moderate success in the United States. This momentum lead Mudhoney to quickly become Sub Pop's flagship band. Mudhoney would also garner respect from contemporaries, and one of the first underground bands of the era to have more success than most, in New York's Sonic Youth. This respect turned into an opening slot on Sonic Youth's UK tour helping spread the word of grunge across the Atlantic.

Superfuzz Bigmuff was an incredibly important record in the history of grunge and alternative music. A few years after its release, Nirvana's Kurt Cobain would list this record as one of his top 50 releases of all time, clearly making it a significant record for the entirety of the scene.

As alternative and grunge music was steadily gaining steam in the underground of American music culture, rap was doing the same thing for its genre as the two fan bases were on a collision course that would aid in the transformation of modern music. A very significant rap album was released in 1988 (August 8th to be exact) which in some ways would help pave the way for its heavy rock distant cousin, grunge, to be accepted by the mainstream later.

N.W.A., the Compton, California band that would launch the careers of Eazy E, Ice Cube, and Dr. Dre, released its debut album, *Straight Outta Compton*, on Eazy E's record label, Ruthless Records, essentially created and brought gangsta rap to the masses. The record would highlight such uncomfortable topics such as drugs, gang violence, police brutality, and the harsh realities of what it was like for black youth growing up in poverty and crime in the inner-city neighborhoods of Los Angeles. MTV played a major role in the mass appeal of N.W.A. with its inclusion of the single, "Express Yourself" into heavy rotation on the network. The album went on to sell over a million copies which at the time took the industry by surprise because this harder, angrier version of rap music was quite different from what was coming out by the more popular East Coast rappers at the time and thus signified change was likely on the way.

With the Seattle music scene still segregated from the rest of the world, commercial music was bathing in a sea of uninspired mediocrity. The Billboard 200 Number One Albums chart of 1989 points to this. Number-one albums throughout the year by artists such as Anita Baker, Bobby Brown, Debbie Gibson, New Kids on the Block, Milli Vanilli, Billy Joel, Phil Collins, and others aren't exactly the type of artists that would be natural lead-ins to heavy, dirty, sludgy, metal/punk rock bands that would take over these very charts in a few short years. The heaviest rock music that enjoyed commercial success were albums by bands like Motley Crue, Guns N' Roses, The Rolling Stones, and Aerosmith. The Red Hot Chili Peppers did make it to 53 with *Mother's Milk* but it didn't make enough noise to signal to the world what was on the horizon.

June 15, 1989, is a landmark date in the history of the Seattle scene as well as music history in general. It was on this date that Sub Pop Records released *Bleach*, the debut album by that little band out of Aberdeen, Washington, Nirvana. No one knew it then, but the record that cost $606.17 for 30 hours of recording (as billed by Jack Endino of Reciprocal Recording Studios) would be the stimulant that led to a change in music and culture that has lasted over thirty years and counting. This moment in time will always be a part of music history for as long as people love and listen to music.

If you're of a certain age, you know the importance of the mixtape. I told a story earlier about how a mixtape changed my life. To revisit what a mixtape is for you unfortunate souls who weren't around to make them yourselves, imagine your digital playlists but with ten times more feeling, passion, and emotion thrown into making them. The reason I say this is because of the physical element that went into the creation of the tape. There was a certain magic in holding the cassette, writing the song titles on those tiny lines inside

CHAPTER 6 - 1988-1990: IT'S ALWAYS DARKEST BEFORE THE DAWN

the cover, and listening intently to the music you were recording because you needed impeccable timing to work the pause, record, and play buttons on the boombox if you planned on getting it right. We took pride in making those tapes and it showed. Occasionally, a tape was made that would help define who you were . . . this is exactly what happened to me.

I brought this up because it was on this mixtape from my friend Pat that I first heard the music of Nirvana. Looking back on this, it's interesting that the song he chose to include on the tape was the softest, most melodic song off *Bleach*. If you know the album, you know it's known for its raw, loud, and distortion-fueled bombast. Yet the song Pat included on my tape was "About a Girl," a Beatle-esque ballad with a touch of angst but nothing like anything else that made it onto Nirvana's debut album. Having never heard of Nirvana before owning this tape, I assumed this was their signature sound. I liked it and I wanted to hear more. When I went to the mall in my neighborhood soon after hearing the song, I was shocked when I heard what *Bleach* (and Nirvana) was all about. Shocked and pleasantly surprised.

Bleach sounded familiar yet brand new all at the same time. With its heavy riffs, pounding drums, and groove-laden low-end bass, it gave me enough Black Sabbath to feel at home but there was a new twist that I couldn't quite identify. There was desperation in the lead singer's scratchy vocals that pulled me in and made me pay very close attention. Kurt Cobain had officially entered my musical consciousness and to date, he's still there.

Important musical movements are usually accompanied by shifts in culture and society. Oftentimes shifts in culture and society become the impetus for new musical movements. Now it's not always obvious but looking back you can easily put the pieces together and see how and why this confluence of events can affect both sides. For me, and some of the world in 1989, we knew some major changes were taking place and underground music was beginning to reflect this.

It's been said that great art is born out of hardship and strife. Music, especially punk rock, hardcore, and hip-hop, has always been a beacon of hope when it comes to artistic expression as it relates to the surroundings of those making the music. This was also typical of folk music in the 1960s which would eventually be dubbed "protest" music. Whether it's war, the economy, or the political climate, the world has always seen opposition from the have-nots toward the haves. 1989 was no different.

The Tiananmen Square protests in Beijing, China from April through the beginning of June '89 against the Communist regime was something the entire world was watching and reacting to. The violent end, with hundreds, if not thousands, dead, had a profound effect on artists worldwide. How could it not? With Communism clearly under siege, a more positive event took place on November 9, 1989. Although the reunification of Germany wouldn't be official until October 3, 1990, the Berlin Wall started coming down when nearly two million people took hammers and chisels to it on November 9, 1989 with the announcement from East German officials that the gates to the wall would now be open to everyone. People of all ages, ethnicities, and nationalities celebrated this monumental event the world over and it was obvious that the world as we knew it would be different forever. Major historical events will always spark creativity and the youth culture will find ways to express their feelings about the world in which they live.

I was sixteen years old when the Berlin Wall came down, just old enough to have a basic understanding of what it all meant. It was an exciting time in history and my generation was coming of age just as the cold war was ending. We no longer had a foreign enemy to hate as our parents had grown up with and there was more optimism with kids my age than what the middle-aged baby boomers had experienced when it came to breaking down walls both literally and figuratively. Culture was just beginning to show signs of what my generation was interested in, but it certainly wasn't in the mainstream yet. I was falling in love with the new music I was listening to more and more each day and something about the sound, feel, and message of what I was hearing

CHAPTER 6 - 1988-1990: IT'S ALWAYS DARKEST BEFORE THE DAWN

was burrowing deep into my soul, creating the young adult I was becoming. It was right around this time that I began to write poetry and/or song lyrics, in black and white marble notebooks daily. I still have those notebooks to this very day but it's difficult to read them. The few times I've gone back and paged through it all, I read about a lost kid who was unhappy with everything in his life with one exception, music.

By 1990, Seattle was already a city to be reckoned with as far as the underground music scene was concerned. Between 1989 and 1990, Seattle/Washington State bands such as Nirvana, Soundgarden, Tad, Mother Love Bone, Mudhoney, Melvins, Alice In Chains, Gruntruck, Skin Yard, Screaming Trees, Green River, and others had records out. Many of the bands and musicians I've already mentioned (and countless others I have not) had made a name for themselves to varying degrees and the first year of this new decade would prove to play a pivotal role in the dominance of the Pacific Northwest would have over music and culture in the coming months and years.

The most significant event was unfortunately also the most tragic. 1990 would see the release of the debut album by Mother Love Bone, the first of the two bands to rise from the ashes of Green River as mentioned a bit earlier in the book. Before we discuss the tragedy that befell the band in 1990, let's look at the promise that was not to be.

In November 1988, Mother Love Bone was signed to Polydor/Stardog Records, a subsidiary of the major label, Polygram Records. Things in the Seattle music scene in '88 and '89 had become white hot by this time as three bands, essentially unknown outside of the Pacific Northwest (Mother Love Bone, Soundgarden, and Alice In Chains) all had major label deals. In March 1989, Mother Love Bone released its debut EP *Shine*. The record sold well, and the future seemed bright for the new group. Interestingly, Mother Love Bone's sound was nothing like the band several of its members came from, Green River. Mudhoney, with its dark, sludgy sound, resembled more of Green River's punk aesthetic, while MLB, leaned on a combination of glam rock and heavy metal. This difference in their sounds is yet another example of why I believe the term grunge should not be considered a sound but instead a title that reflects a musical and cultural period.

Slated to be released in March of 1990, *Apple* was one of the most anticipated albums of the year because the band consisted of such underground luminaries as previously noted. Unfortunately, this was when tragedy struck. Mother Love Bone's gregarious and one-of-a-kind lead singer, Andrew Wood, overdosed on heroin on March 16, 1990, just days before the scheduled release of *Apple*. Wood was no stranger to drugs as he'd already been in rehab a few times trying to overcome his addiction. After two days in the hospital, being kept alive on life support, Andy Wood died from his overdose. He was only twenty-four years old.

With Wood's untimely and unexpected death, Mother Love Bone would delay the release of its debut album for a bit and release it on July 19, 1990, via Stardog/Mercury Records. The band's music was a big departure from the punk and metal-infused Green River and took on more of a glam rock style more fitting of Wood's vocal style and larger-than-life personality. Many who heard and saw Mother Love Bone perform were confident that they were destined to become the breakout band that Seattle was seemingly steamrolling toward creating.

In October of 1990, Kim Neely of *Rolling Stone Magazine* said, "Mother Love Bone's debut album succeeds where countless other hard-rock albums have failed, capturing the essence of what made Zep immortal—dynamics, kids!—and giving it a unique Nineties spin. "Stardog Champion" has the chugging, bluesy appeal of "When the Levee Breaks;" numbers like "Crown of Thorns" echo with the sadness that marked "The Rain Song;" the guitar on psychedelic rave-ups like "This Is Shangri-La" is loose, unruly and blissfully imperfect. *Apple* is nothing short of a masterpiece."

As tragic as the death of Andrew Wood was, it also set into motion the events that would go on to create one of the biggest bands, not just of the

CHAPTER 6 - 1988-1990: IT'S ALWAYS DARKEST BEFORE THE DAWN

era, but in the history of music. In the immediate wake of Wood's passing though, two of his Mother Love Bone bandmates, Jeff Ament and Stone Gossard, along with Andy's former roommate and Soundgarden frontman, Chris Cornell, would form the one-off album and group (along with future Pearl Jam guitarist Mike McCready, singer Eddie Vedder, and current Soundgarden and future Pearl Jam drummer, Matt Cameron), Temple of the Dog. This would happen as the group I referred to as one of the biggest in history was also taking shape, Pearl Jam. Out of tragedy can arise triumph and in the case of the early '90s Seattle music scene, and eventually the world over, that is exactly what took place. I was lucky enough to speak with someone who was not only there for it all, but instrumental in shaping what was to come.

Eileen Mercolino, the Chief Marketing Officer at *Spin* magazine at the time of our interview, was on hand and directing traffic during those post-Mother Love Bone, pre–Pearl Jam days.

"Not many people know this about my history," said Mercolino, "but I introduced Eddie Vedder to Stone and Jeff. Eddie was a close friend of mine, along with Beth (Eddie's first wife) as we were interns at Virgin Records (the record label) together. I was back and forth a lot between San Diego and Los Angeles back then, and always very enterprising. I'd stay with Beth and Eddie at their place, or they would stay with me at mine. Eddie's favorite band back then was the Red Hot Chili Peppers and he became friends with Jack Irons (the Pepper's drummer at the time) from working local shows down in San Diego."

Mercolino shared so many details about that time. I was drawn in. "When Beth and I graduated, I got a job at Polygram Records and Beth stayed at Virgin. One of the projects I was working on for Polygram was the Mother Love Bone record. I was an assistant, so I was doing all the hotel and meeting arrangements, etc., and Stone and Jeff had to promote the record, but this was after Andy (Andrew Wood) had died so they weren't all that happy about it. Eddie had told me through Jack Irons that they (Stone and

Jeff) were forming another band, and they were going to leave with Michael Goldstone (an executive at Polygram) and go to Epic Records. It was this big secret, but Jack knew because they had wanted him to be the drummer in that new band. So, Jeff and Stone had come into the office one day and Jack had previously said something to them about Eddie being this great singer (in addition to needing a drummer for their new group, they also needed a singer) and they should meet him. They were like, 'ok, but we really want you to be our drummer.'"

When Stone and Jeff came in to meet with Eileen, she referenced the connection with Jack Irons and recommended they meet with Eddie. They asked her if this guy played basketball. She said he did, and they asked her to have Eddie give them a call so they could meet up, talk, and shoot hoops together. Eileen agreed and as soon as Jeff and Stone left, she immediately called Eddie.

"Listen, dude, you need to get your ass up here (to L.A.) because I just told Stone and Jeff that you were in town and that later today, you'd be available to meet them and play some basketball. So, whatever you need to do, do it and just get it together."

The meeting and basketball game did take place. When Eileen asked Eddie how it went, he said that it went well, and they were going to send him a tape of some music to listen to. If you know the history of Pearl Jam and this tape sounds familiar to you, it should. The tape turned out to be the infamous "Mommason" tape that included the music to what would become the songs, "Alive," "Once," and "Footsteps" that Eddie listened to, went surfing to digest what he had heard, and then went back, recorded vocals over, and sent back to Jeff.

This cassette, this random piece of plastic and tape, would essentially become the first, unofficial Pearl Jam demo, and three decades later, not only is the band still around, but countless people (yours truly included) have been following, chronicling, writing about, and listening to them for almost all that time. Eileen, though, had a jump on the rest of us when it came to

CHAPTER 6 - 1988-1990: IT'S ALWAYS DARKEST BEFORE THE DAWN

hearing the music that millions the world over would soon fall in love with.

Mercolino was ahead of her time. She shared, "I remember him (Eddie) playing me the tape in some car before sending it off to Jeff and Stone and I told him, 'This is fucking amazing.'" You weren't wrong, Eileen, you weren't wrong.

If there's a "Big Four" of popular grunge bands from the early '90s, they would be Soundgarden, Nirvana, Pearl Jam, and Alice in Chains. For the most part, these are the bands people associate with the grunge movement, at least commercially, and are easily identifiable by their unique styles and sounds. None of these bands sound alike, a popular misnomer by people who think grunge is a sound, but it is not. It's an aesthetic and a period perhaps, but not a sound. I've always suggested to people who debate this that they should listen to these bands in succession and after they do, tell me if they sound alike. I think it's more than likely that what they'll hear is the heavy metal sounds mixed with experimental/psychedelic influences of Soundgarden, the raw but catchy-as-hell punk of Nirvana, the '70s-influenced hard rock with the punk attitude of the Ramones in Pearl Jam, and the sludgy, guitar riff-heavy metal of Black Sabbath in Alice In Chains. Grunge is a label to help identify and discuss loud Seattle rock music from the early 1990s, but if you've paid attention to the music from that time, you'd understand how different most bands were.

Facelift, released by Columbia Records on August 21, 1990, was the debut, full-length album from Alice in Chains. Combining Black Sabbath-like riffs with hauntingly beautiful vocals, harmonies, and melodies, *Facelift* is certainly one of the first albums from the era that captured the mood and atmosphere that is still associated with grunge to this very day, at least on a large, commercial scale. Like most of the early Seattle bands that were responsible for starting the grunge movement, the members of Alice in Chains had been on the local scene in different bands going back to the early and mid-'80s. Lead singer, Layne Staley, a drummer by trade, found himself singing in a glam-rock band called Sleze in 1984 and met the guitarist of the band

Diamond Lie, Jerry Cantrell in 1987. With bassist Mike Starr and drummer Sean Kinney, both regulars in the mid-'80s Seattle music scene as well, Alice in Chains, with this lineup, officially formed in 1987.

The truth is, *Facelift* was a monumentally important release as it was the first record from the newly termed "grunge" bands to have a gold and platinum-selling album. In many ways, it paved the way for the mass appeal and acceptance the music from Seattle would garner all over the world once other releases came out. Nirvana's *Nevermind* just feels like it was destined to do magical things regardless of what came before it, but there's an argument to be made that without the earlier success of *Facelift*, the Seattle scene could have taken longer to catch on commercially or even more interestingly, perhaps it wouldn't have caught on at all. Luckily, we have *Facelift* so we will never know how things would have transpired without it, but it's certainly a thought-provoking conversation.

As with any new shift in culture, it's rarely the first people who do the things that become popular, who get recognized for them first. They usually do get their props, as Alice In Chains is a shining example of, but it's typically the ones who are right behind those who were there first but couldn't quite cross the goal line, that score game-winning touchdowns. As *Facelift* would gain steam in late 1990, it started to officially take off in early 1991 with the release of the single and video for the track, "Man in the Box."

If grunge wasn't a household name yet (it wasn't) this video would go a long way toward changing that. The video shows the band performing in an old, dirty, dingy barn situated on what looks to be a rundown farm. Throughout the video, a mysterious man wearing a black hooded cloak is shown roaming around the grounds. As the video is coming to an end, the hooded man reveals himself, and we learn that his eyelids were sewn together the whole time. This is a depiction of the line in the song, *"Feed my eyes, now you've sewn them shut."* Using a sepia tone, the video was shot on 16mm film which gives the video its dark, gritty, dare I say, grungy, feel to it. And that feel was just what this undercover poet needed.

CHAPTER 6 – 1988-1990: IT'S ALWAYS DARKEST BEFORE THE DAWN

What was coming out of Seattle in 1990 was dark and had substance. This music was still very much underground. The pop charts, though, told a different story that music wasn't dangerous; it didn't challenge anyone or anything. It was void of any social or political themes. It was soulless. It was bland. Some of these songs were of course very well written as songwriting goes, and they often displayed catchy melodies and pretty vocals and there's nothing wrong with that. If you were looking for meaning, inspiration, or salvation in your music though, if you were looking for the next revolution, popular music throughout the '80s and into the very early '90s wasn't where you were going to find it.

To showcase what I'm saying, let's look at the Billboard 200 for some historical guidance for the periods right before, during, and after the release of *Nevermind* by Nirvana on September 24th, 1991, by DGC Records.

The year before *Nevermind* came out, during the very same week, the Top 10 artists (in order) whose albums topped the Billboard 200 were as follows:

Week of September 22nd, 1990:

M.C. Hammer, Wilson Phillips, Jon Bon Jovi, Mariah Carey, Bell Biv DeVoe, Prince, Poison, Anita Baker, Keith Sweat, and Michael Bolton.

If I were looking to start a musical revolution, this is not the list of artists I'd enlist… just sayin'. I take that back. I would have Prince be a part of the revolution, but everyone else, no chance. Prince was one of the most gifted, talented, and unique musicians who ever lived. He was a genius, and his untimely death in 2016, left a void in music that cannot be properly filled. As a matter of fact, in the year following his death (Prince died on April 21, 2016), according to Nielsen Music, Prince sold a combined 7.7 million copies of his songs and albums in the U.S. alone. That was more than any other artist during that same time. Simply astounding. So, Prince is more than welcome in my army.

If you're not familiar with some or all the artists on this list, here's why I wouldn't have them fighting my revolution… you may feel otherwise…who knows? M.C. Hammer, the Oakland A's ball boy turned rapper, wore baggy pants probably three sizes too big and shuffled across the stage while performing his gigantic hit, "Can't Touch This." Great for him, not so much for my infantry. Jon Bon Jovi is successful beyond all recognition, but musically, not exactly the bulldog I'd want on the front lines. Wilson Phillips, a supergroup of sorts, was the offspring of the legendary Brian Wilson of the Beach Boys and the daughter of John and Michelle Phillips of the Mammas and the Papas. Pop music gold, but edgy is not in their vocabulary. As far as Michael Bolton is concerned, well, you can just figure that one out for yourself.

CHAPTER 7 – 1991
THE EXPLOSION: WE HAVE LIFTOFF

"WHY THE HELL WOULD YOU WANT TO JOIN ONE OF THOSE PROTESTS? AREN'T YOU AN AMERIcan?" said one of my uncles upon learning that my friends and I were discussing the possibility that we'd go to an anti-war demonstration relating to Operation Desert Storm and the Gulf War once the U.S.-led coalition began an aerial bombing campaign in Iraq in mid-January 1991.

"If I go it's because I am an American," I said proudly. "The great thing about this country is that we have the freedom to speak our minds and if protesting is how we do it, so be it." The conversation ebbed and flowed and as most politically and culturally driven conversations go, we didn't change the other person's mind and probably looked at one another a bit differently going forward. I'm not saying that it's right or the most mature resolution, but I was a kid about to leave high school and go to college and my uncle was a retired military officer so was there another outcome to be had? Not likely.

After this exchange, I remember feeling even more distanced and misunderstood by adults in my world than ever before. This wasn't the cause of that feeling, I'd been heading down that path for quite some time by this point, but it was more proof that I needed to follow the road I intuitively knew was mine to walk. The early '90s wasn't only a sea change for music and youth culture, but they were my time to become who I needed to be. I was ready.

Throughout history, some years wind up becoming more important than others. That happens when certain years collide with specific cultural phenomena and become seared into the souls of those who were there to witness it all. When culture and music collide, those events tend to be remembered, not only by those who were there but also by those who were lucky enough to have the music passed down to them from those who lived it.

Sticking with music as an example, when we see "1956" many people will think of Elvis Presley and the "birth" of rock 'n' roll . Just like every genre before though, rock 'n' roll wasn't invented by the ones who made it popular or commercially viable. Elvis's white skin and movie star good looks allowed America to sell this new music knowing damn well they couldn't sell the truth about where the music came from and who created it. Good luck convincing 1950s mainstream America to buy records made by black Southerners who created this new sound.

Most people will have a similar Pavlovian response when discussing music and having the year 1964 brought up. "The British Invasion" of the United States was (and still is) one of the most important cultural events to occur in modern times. This was the year that folks outside of a small, port town in a borough tucked away in the Northwestern end of England called Liverpool, met The Beatles. With bands such as The Rolling Stones, The Yardbirds, The Kinks, Donovan, and others right behind, the British Invasion was in full swing. Musically speaking, the massive cultural bombs dropped in the mid-'50s and mid-'60s are still looked upon as a sacred ground for artistic and societal high-water marks.

As I write this almost seven decades after Elvis first shook those hips, many music fans still understand and reference the importance of 1956. The same thing happens when mentioning 1964, and to a lesser degree, if 1977 is mentioned, you will hear people immediately start talking about the be-

CHAPTER 7 - 1991: THE EXPLOSION

ginnings of punk rock. For the entirety of my childhood, those were the only years on the Mt. Rushmore of years when music created culture and influenced their respective generations, creating lifelong fans, and leaving its imprint on the souls and minds of those hit with it all. That was the case until 1991.

As I've discussed throughout the book thus far, grunge and alternative music did not happen by accident, nor was it created overnight with 1991 being its birth year. Instead, it was the boiling point created out of decades of musical boredom, cultural insignificance, and popular music that refused to push a single boundary. Nirvana's "Smells Like Teen Spirit" should have surprised no one but because few people were paying attention, it surprised everyone.

It's not easy to describe what it was like when "Smells Like Teen Spirit" was released, particularly the music video accompanying it, but it was the sonic (and visual) equivalent of an earthquake, hurricane, and volcanic eruption happening simultaneously changing the landscape of everything in its path forever. Outside of Seattle, there weren't many of us who knew who Nirvana was before their meteoric rise to fame on the heels of *Nevermind*, but even for those of us who knew who they were, no one could predict they would become the biggest band on the planet and one of the most important bands in music history. No one.

"Smells Like Teen Spirit" was officially released as the first single off *Nevermind* on September 10th, 1991. It was given to radio shortly before this on August 27th. Record companies typically release songs with a solid plan and strategy in mind, this release was no different. Nirvana's label DGC Records, (their first major label after beginning their career with Sub Pop Records) had the intention of releasing "Teen Spirit" to both strengthen their current fan base in the Pacific Northwest and expand on it. Then, the plan was to release "Come as You Are" as the main single due to what the record company saw as its "crossover to the mainstream" potential. Well, you know what they say about the best-laid plans of mice and men.

There's something you need to know or remember (depending on your age) about music promotion during the late '80s and early '90s. Aside from radio play and album sales, though both were incredibly important factors in whether or not a band or artist would make it, music videos, specifically music videos being played on MTV, were probably the most important factors in determining the success of a song or artist. MTV was still relatively new (it launched on August 1st, 1981) in 1989 when Nirvana released their first album (to relative obscurity), *Bleach* on Sub Pop Records. Despite its newness, it was quickly becoming one of the most important marketing tools for bands to use for commercial success. If your video was in any kind of regular rotation on the channel, you were likely going to become a star, that's the way it was. This certainly held true even ten years after the music channel was born. MTV was perhaps the biggest force in shaping and shifting culture by the time *Nevermind* was released.

The reality is, despite "Smells Like Teen Spirit" being an all-time great rock song, its timing was impeccable. A perfect storm was brewing and Nirvana, along with their debut single off *Nevermind*, were destined to become the eye of that storm. If you think about it, great music by itself, rarely, if ever, can start a cultural revolution. So many outside factors, most having little or nothing to do with the music itself, play massive roles in birthing that revolution. The world is a strange place with many strange things happening in it. When those strange things get stranger or just played out, and the youth of any generation decides it's time for a change, things tend to happen. Add a corrupt political and societal climate, oppression of any kind to a group (or groups) of people, as well as the stifling of true creativity, and finally, radio towers blasting music without much meaning to the masses, and that, my friends, is a recipe for a cultural revolution. All of this, in one form or another, was occurring just as Nirvana had released *Nevermind* and the kids responded

CHAPTER 7 - 1991: THE EXPLOSION

the way they always do during times like these, with raised fists and loud screams of rebellion.

Part of my conversation with Jared Miller about his days booking and promoting bands in NYC in the early '90s centered around when he first thought that things were about to change.

"We were booking 50-60 bands a week in New York City. I had to become familiar with all different styles of music, and I became fascinated with grunge bands," Jared said. "The song that grabbed me and made it all happen was Soundgarden's 'Hands All Over' (off the band's 1989 album, *Louder Than Love*). That was the song that just changed everything for me. So, we started working with a lot of grunge and alternative bands and the record companies liked us because of it. They also liked that we would only book original music, we would not book cover bands. We helped them and they helped us. They gave us all their new videos and releases before they came out to play in the clubs. One of those was 'Smells Like Teen Spirit.' We put it on the jukebox before it was released, and that moment was defining. The place went bananas! It was at Desmond's Tavern and the place just went nuts! Right at that moment for us, the world changed."

It would be difficult for one band to carry the torch for an entire generation, let alone a brand-new genre of music. Most of us didn't know it at the time, but there were so many brilliant and ultimately gigantically important albums that were released in 1991 that it easily goes down in history as one of the best years ever for music. Grunge and alternative may have been at the forefront of what was being released in '91 but they weren't the only genres that broke through and changed the status quo. Hard Rock, Hip-Hop, Heavy Metal, Punk, and Shoegaze music were all present and accounted for in this new world order of music and culture.

Looking back at it now, the bands that released massively important records in 1991 are a who's who list of some of the biggest names in the music industry. Some have gone on to gain entrance into the Rock 'n' Roll Hall of Fame as well. At the time though, most of these bands had little more than the local following from the towns and cities they came from. There's something to be said for being there to witness the birth of a scene and have a front-row seat for the entirety of new careers, and it's quite another thing to stay on the ride with all who lasted more than three decades later.

The list of important albums released in 1991 is very long but also incredibly worthy of mention. I'll dive into some of them as we go but I wanted to acknowledge the records I believe had the biggest impact on the burgeoning music scene. From a musical and cultural standpoint, things would never be the same for the following artists and those coming of age in the early and mid-'90s. My list, in no order, is as follows:

- ✓ *Nevermind* – Nirvana
- ✓ *Ten* - Pearl Jam
- ✓ *Badmotorfinger* – Soundgarden
- ✓ *Temple of the Dog* - Temple of the Dog
- ✓ *Every Good Boy Deserves Fudge* – Mudhoney
- ✓ *Gish* - The Smashing Pumpkins
- ✓ *Trompe le Monde* – Pixies
- ✓ *The Low End Theory* - A Tribe Called Quest
- ✓ *Loveless* - My Bloody Valentine
- ✓ *Blood Sugar Sex Magik* - Red Hot Chili Peppers
- ✓ *Out of Time* - R.E.M.
- ✓ *Use Your Illusion I & II* - Guns N' Roses
- ✓ *Sailing the Seas of Cheese* – Primus
- ✓ *Steady Diet of Nothing* – Fugazi
- ✓ *Achtung Baby* - U2
- ✓ *2Pacalypse Now* - Tupac Shakur
- ✓ *Green Mind* - Dinosaur Jr.
- ✓ *Metallica (aka The Black Album)* – Metallica

CHAPTER 7 - 1991: THE EXPLOSION

- ✓ *Cypress Hill - Cypress Hill*
- ✓ *Mental Jewelry - Live*, and
- ✓ the list goes on...

I chose these releases because they run the gamut of everything I believe 1991 to be about. We've got hugely popular and financially successful albums, culture-shifting records that turned previously unknown artists into global superstars, and confirmation that a relatively new genre like hip-hop was never a fad and would soon become one of the biggest and most influential styles of music ever created, recognition of the earliest scene influencers who maybe didn't get the credit they deserved, and older bands that stayed true to their sound and still flourished (and became bigger) in the wake of grunge and alternative music rising to the biggest heights music and culture can bestow. It was a great fucking year!

As an eighteen-year-old kid who recently graduated high school and was staring down the barrel of a college career I wanted no part of, 1991 was a turning point for me, and not always in the best ways. I've always believed that asking teenagers who can barely take care of themselves while still living in their parent's homes to decide what they want to be when they grow up was always a flawed idea. All these years later, I still feel as strongly, if not stronger, about that take. It's a lot to ask of a kid who is still trying to figure out who they are as a person and what moves them to the point of mapping out the next 60 years of their lives. I, for one, was still clueless.

In August of 1991, I began my freshman year as a Communications major at St. John's University in New York. I think I was always a bit of an underdog in life and even the decision about where I attended college may prove that theory right. At that time, St. John's had two campuses, one in Queens and one in the smallest borough of New York, Staten Island. The Queens campus had about 20,000 students which wasn't something I was comfortable with. The Staten Island campus, in comparison, had just a few thousand which sounded way more appealing to me. I had come from a very small grammar school, and a small high school, so keeping that tradition alive felt right to me. I sacrificed the bigger, more prestigious campus and decided to go with the smaller and barely known "step" campus. It was par for my course.

As it turned out, choosing the smaller, less popular campus was the right decision. Many factors contributed to that truth, the most important being my eventual inclusion in the local Staten Island underground music scene. This happened as organically as things like this tend to happen . . . fashion. Allow me to explain.

Back in 1991, most of the culture and fashion from the 1980s was still spilling over into the new and yet undefined decade. This meant lots of gold chains and tracksuits for the guys and plenty of high hair and oversized sweatshirts for the girls. Most kids my age dressed this way but as usual, a small but dedicated minority typically referred to as the "underground" existed. This is where I fit in.

One day, as I walked into a large classroom with at least 50 students, I scanned my surroundings for any signs of folks like me. I wasn't having any luck. As I stood there with my long hair, Jane's Addiction t-shirt, jeans, and black construction boots, I was quickly losing hope that I'd find a kindred spirit. Then it happened . . . peering through a sea of Sergio Tacchini and Aqua Net, I noticed a figure on the other side of the room that stood out amongst the nonsense. He was dressed almost identically to me with the minor exception of the band on his t-shirt. Proudly displaying the Misfits logo on a black shirt, I knew this was the only person in the room I would fit in with. Not coincidentally, we managed to choose the same row to sit in, finally grabbing a spot, a seat or two from one another. This would mark the beginning of my introduction to the Staten Island music scene and a life-long friendship.

In August of 1990, the United States, with George H. Bush as President

CHAPTER 7 - 1991: THE EXPLOSION

and a coalition of over 40 other countries, led a military build-up against Iraq called Operation Desert Shield, eventually evolving into Operation Desert Storm, which began with an aerial bombing campaign in Iraq on January 17, 1991. During this period, I was still in high school and along with everyone else my age, facing an uncertain future. We no longer were only having discussions of which colleges we were attending or what types of careers we were planning, but now, we contemplated the idea of possibly being drafted and going to war.

This may sound extreme to those who were not eighteen or about to turn eighteen in 1990 or 1991, but the talk around the country in high schools in every neighborhood was loud and it was wrought with fear. We had only known the draft to be something we read about in history books or stories from our fathers and grandfathers. In my case, I was reminded of how my father enlisted in the Army during the Vietnam War just so he wouldn't get drafted. It was common back then that if you enlisted, you had a better chance of not deploying to the front lines and serving in another location in a non-infantry capacity. In my dad's situation, he was sent to Korea as a Specialist Teletype Operator with Crypto Secret Clearance. He never did travel to Vietnam and he's still alive today. He believes had he been drafted, his situation would have been extremely less favorable.

With all of this in mind, and many of my friends having similar stories, we thought a draft was imminent. With no social media back then, all our information was received via local and national news outlets such as television, newspapers, and radio. U.S. government officials were quick to quell our fears but the language they used in doing so was murky at best.

"We prefer the all-volunteer Army," said Lt. Cmdr. Edward Lundquist, a then Pentagon Spokesperson. "We're not expecting to go back to the draft."

I do not see a *"no"* in there anywhere. I see words like *"prefer"* and *"not expecting."* I may have only been a teenager but I was smart enough to not trust those with that kind of power, especially when using vague language that leaves the door open to change everything that was originally said.

The Secretary of State during this time, Dick Cheney, used even more telling language when he addressed the Senate Armed Services Committee in December of 1990 concerning the possibility of draft reinstatement by saying, "Obviously, at some point, if you were going to stay for an extended period, you're going to want to come back and address anew, the question of rotation policy." Once again, not a *"no"* in sight.

While this White House was run by a Republican President, the Democrats jumped right into the non-committal language gymnastics concerning the draft when Senator Sam Nunn (D) of Georgia said, "We've always known from the very beginning of the volunteer force that, if we got into a large conflict, particularly ground conflict, we were going to have a draft." I rest my case.

My generation was seriously concerned about what the immediate, and possibly deadly, future held for us. We had ourselves to turn to and discuss all the possible scenarios, but that wasn't enough, at least not for me. I turned to music and writing as an escape. As the rest of 1991 would start to play out, the Gulf War would end abruptly on February 28th with the liberation of Kuwait. Crisis averted for the moment, but the thoughts, feelings, and emotions of a generation had been forever changed and the proof of this would reveal itself in just a few short months from the end of the war.

I've been covering and writing about '90s music for about twenty years and one thing that remains constant is how this music is the lifeblood of millions of people worldwide. Nirvana certainly wasn't the only band from that era that created this raging passion, but they were the biggest.

There aren't many bands that last over thirty years, let alone release an album with the historical impact that Nirvana did with *Nevermind*, released on September 24, 1991. This is the record that was the impetus for everything in the grunge and alternative world that followed.

CHAPTER 7 - 1991: THE EXPLOSION

It's not an everyday occurrence, to say the least. Even with all the time that has passed, Nirvana is still gaining fans and taking its place in the cultural consciousness well into the 2020s. The songs on *Nevermind*, many of which became at the time, and are still today, iconic, were the initial guiding forces to the new and radical music and culture phenomenon throughout the '90s.

It's obvious that "Smells Like Teen Spirit" is the song that represents Nirvana the most, and it's easy to understand why. It's the song that started the most important musical movement since The Beatles landed in New York in 1964.

I have news for you though, in many people's opinion (as subjective as that may be) it's not the best song on *Nevermind*.

A bit of a hot take for some I'm sure, but I will explain. I, along with millions of others, loved "Smells Like Teen Spirit" from the first moment I heard that jangly guitar riff, leading to the gut-punch that is Dave Grohl's massive drum explosion, the stage was set. The song sounded like nothing that was out at the time. The soft-to-loud dynamic that Nirvana had perfected (thanks to the Pixies) acted like a sonic addiction. A nation of slackers suddenly became disciples of the trio from Seattle with their stage as our altar.

Nevermind satisfied a need we weren't aware we had. The band acted, and we reacted. The harmonious marriage has now lasted over thirty years and guided the misguided all along the way. Songs like "In Bloom" and "Come as You Are" were built for radio play. Both were instantaneously memorable, utilizing that verse/chorus/verse, soft-to-loud formula perfected on "Teen Spirit." The songwriter living inside of Kurt Cobain took every punk and pop melodic sensibility he had, added distortion, a pained growl, and essentially created a monster. We still can't get enough.

"Breed" is the heaviest song at this point on the record. It reminds us that Nirvana is here to be fast and loud above all else. Placing it fourth on the track listing was a great move.

Next up we have "Lithium". By now it's safe to say Nirvana is unapologetically using its classic formula of sound dynamics and we've fully bought in.

On their debut album Bleach, Nirvana has a song called "About A Girl", which is as close as that record gets to having an acoustic track on it. As I've discussed previously, it's the song that first introduced me to the band back in 1989. I bring that up because "Polly", the sixth song on *Nevermind* is in fact an acoustic song, the first one we hear on the album. Its haunting atmosphere and dark lyrics are something Nirvana would become known for in their short-lived career.

"Territorial Pissings" is a blazing, fuzzed-infused punk song. Grohl hits the drums on this song as if his life depended on it and Kurt's voice is scratchy, desperate, and vulnerable at the same time. If you weren't sold on *Nevermind*'s power by this point in the record, perhaps this music isn't for you.

The Pixies' influence and sound dynamic is back in full force on "Drain You", one of the album's catchiest songs.

Remember when I said that "Smells Like Teen Spirit" isn't the best song on *Nevermind*? And remember when you thought I was crazy for suggesting it? Well, in my humble opinion, we've arrived at the best song on the album. "Lounge Act" has everything in it that makes Nirvana great. To me, it's their most perfectly crafted song. From the first notes of Krist Novoselic's bassline, setting up the rhythm for the song, "Lounge Act" already feels like something special. Kurt's vocals are clear and understated. This song oozes melody as the first verse leads into the chorus seamlessly.

After the first verse, you may be left wondering why I think it's so good. It's nothing you haven't heard before. Even as the second verse plays after the first chorus, you may not realize what's going on. It sounds almost identical to the first. If you listen closely though, this song has that subtle magic so many great songs have...it creates anticipation. The tempo never changes, the chords never change, but there's a slow and steady shift in the feeling coming from Kurt's voice. If you haven't noticed it before, you will after reading this.

CHAPTER 7 - 1991: THE EXPLOSION

Then, the third verse happens...

This verse is Nirvana. This is the kind of emotion few songs can deliver with nothing but a vocal change. The sheer desperation and angst in Kurt's voice crashes through the speakers and covers the listener in the magic that is music. He was leading us here the entire time. He understood the power of dynamics more than just about anyone and this verse is the greatest payoff on the album.

"Stay Away" and "On A Plain" are more of the same in terms of the quiet/loud formula that has kicked our collective ass throughout the record thus far. This album was designed with songs like these in mind and they deliver in a big way.

One of, if not the most important albums of the last three decades ends with a poetic drone that may just be the most honest look into the soul of Kurt Cobain. With what sounds like a pawn shop-purchased acoustic guitar, "Something in the Way" plods along with a barely audible Kurt singing in a whisper. We heard the haunting tones of "Polly" earlier, but this track is as haunting as it gets. It's somber and brutal but beautiful at the same time.

So much has changed since September 24, 1991. Looking back, I can't understand how three decades have passed since this generation-defining album was released. But they have.

Kurt had a love/hate relationship with his fame, so I often wonder how he'd view this album now had he lived. If I had the chance to ask him about the impact this album had on the world then and now, something tells me his answer might have been... "oh well, whatever, nevermind".

Conservative numbers show that *Nevermind* has sold over 30 million copies (Nirvana overall boasts more than 75 million albums sold in total), billions of streams, and generations of fans. Nirvana, (as well as their groundbreaking album *Nevermind*), will be lauded as one of the best-selling and most influential bands and albums of all time.

September 29, 1991, was a very significant date in the history of the grunge and alternative movement as it marks, in my opinion, the event that caused the entire scene to blow up and eventually create a new musical revolution that is still flourishing over 30 years later. Although Nirvana's *Nevermind* was released five days earlier on September 24th, and Pearl Jam's *Ten* was released nearly a month earlier on August 27th (both records would go on to define the entire scene commercially), September 29th was the day the fuse was lit before all hell broke loose.

On that date, the music video for "Smells Like Teen Spirit," the lead single off Nirvana's second album (first on a major label), debuted on MTV's "underground" show 120 Minutes. I believe that Nirvana would still become huge, and the scene would eventually make its mark in music history, but without that video, at that time, I'm not sure that things would've changed as drastically as they did. As mentioned earlier, the time was right for a musical and cultural change.

With commercial music not pushing the envelope, kids becoming disillusioned with life in a new decade, and an uncertain future with war and an unstable economy being the norm, sounds and lyrics coming mainly from the Pacific Northwest were needed and would've found a hole in society to break through regardless. That video though, featuring three grimy and dirty-looking musicians, wild and reckless kids moshing and slam dancing with gothic-looking cheerleaders less than enthusiastically encouraging, and an old janitor seemingly breaking free from the chains of a boring existence due to the music and chaos around him, all while a high school gymnasium was being destroyed, was exactly what my generation needed to take off.

Keep in mind, MTV as a network was only ten years old in '91 and they didn't take many chances regarding the types of videos they played during the day. It was a steady diet of Michael Jackson, Madonna, Bruce Springsteen, Duran Duran, and the like.

Nirvana consisted of three completely unknown musicians with a song that sounded like nothing on Top 40 radio then. They weren't about to take a

CHAPTER 7 - 1991: THE EXPLOSION

chance on something so outrageous at the time. That's where a program like *120 Minutes* comes in.

When the show began in 1986 it catered to "alternative music", mostly European artists like Morrisey, The Jesus and Mary Chain, New Order, and so on. It was created by British journalist, producer, and DJ, Dave Kendall who wanted to showcase the bands and music he loved. As time moved on, American artists such as Butthole Surfers, Dinosaur Jr., Bad Religion, etc., were getting airtime on the program as well. If you had access to cable television in the Mid-80s (not everyone did as they do now) and could stay up late enough to watch *120 Minutes*, you started to sense something cool was happening.

When *120 Minutes* aired "Smells Like Teen Spirit" in the early Fall of '91, it was another spoke in what was about to become a massive wheel, rolling and spinning completely out of control down a hill as big as planet earth. With rock music finding its way, slowly but surely, onto the charts and MTV hitting its stride, underground music, once reserved for college radio and outcasts around the country, was soon to become a musical and cultural force that would change everything.

I could remember thinking at the time of that infamous cassette tape from my friend Pat I mentioned earlier in the book, and me being a fan of *120 Minutes*, that this new music was not only great, but it was mine. The world at large didn't know it existed, and I liked it that way. I was a part of a secret club, a sonic membership, and only a select few were lucky enough or worthy enough to know about and have.

When you're young and feel like you don't belong in or to the world at large, the world your parents and teachers taught you about, you look for something else. You find your tribe and you do anything and everything possible to keep your membership in good standing. This is your world now and it's time to find that tribe and stake your claim in it. When I watched *120 Minutes* or listened to that cassette, or tuned into some fuzzy-sounding college radio station, I was where I was supposed to be. My friends were images on a screen, music coming through speakers and headphones, along with words on the pages of magazines and fanzines from around the world. Record store owners were mayors and governors—musical lawmakers who told you what's what, and you didn't question it. You gleefully obliged and went back for more.

Most people in your daily life had no clue about this alternate universe, or this double life you were leading, but it existed. It was real and it was about to get much, much bigger.

Thinking back on those times now, I can't help but remember the people I was around and the musical landscape that existed then. When we think about our past many questions get answered concerning who we are. We can learn a lot about why we think the way we do now or why we like the things we like. We see all the little crumbs and clues about our past (and the decisions we made), and how they turned into the large bricks that paved the way to our future selves. Oftentimes we take for granted all the influences that found their way into our souls and created the blueprint for how we turned out. Music did that for me. I'd imagine if you're reading this book, it did the same thing for you as well.

Videos were so important to the success of bands/artists throughout the '80s/'90s, most of us living through those times took it for granted. MTV was not only the largest cultural tastemaker where musicians were concerned, but so many of the people who worked at the network back then became influential in the music industry, television, fashion, marketing, and overall entertainment. Many of the people I've interviewed for this book got their start at MTV yet never knew one another. This includes Psytrance music artist, VJ Baby K. Psytrance is a subgenre of trance music consisting of rhythms and layered melodies created by high-tempo riffs.

VJ Baby K, or Kristina Marie as she's known to her colleagues and clients around the world, is a high-level marketing professional with such names as

CHAPTER 7 - 1991: THE EXPLOSION

Barclays, Amazon, Shopify, IMAN, Yura Agency, and others to her credit. Music was always embedded in Kristina's DNA as her very first "real" job demonstrates.

"I was a segment producer for MTV Asia in the early '90s and had the privilege of interviewing artists such as David Bowie, Chris Cornell, and Dave Grohl," said Kristina when we spoke from her home in Barcelona.

We discussed the importance of MTV and the visual aspect of music in the late '80s/early '90s and Kristina had a front-row seat and perspective on it all. She understands implicitly why the video for "Smells Like Teen Spirit" was so important to Nirvana's and the scene's overall success.

She said, "Music is what I kept latching onto back then ('90/'91) and I fell into marketing around the same time. The world was extremely kind to me and provided me with the soul-saving aspects of music that we all have. During this time there was a new demand placed upon musicians. You now needed MTV. You've got to have a music video. It was quite palpable. The feeling was there was this new form of getting people to know your soul and how that looks on video. It's no longer just about how you sound, your lyrics, or how well you recorded your songs with your band. There's now this next layer."

It may be difficult to imagine in today's world, but back in 1991, MTV not only played music videos all day long, but the videos they played almost always helped the bands who made those videos become superstars. The internet was in its infancy and social media wasn't even a glimmer in the eyes of Silicon Valley. Radio airplay, MTV, record store sales, and promotions were the order of the day. When MTV deemed you a star, the world took notice. Some people think Nirvana was an overnight sensation and this wasn't true. As I've already discussed earlier in the book, this music and the bands, including Nirvana, who created this revolution, had been brewing for years.

By December of 1991, the world knew who Nirvana was. *Nevermind* had gone from its debut position at #144 on the Billboard 200 in September, to #6 on the list for the week of December 21st. This wasn't like Metallica or Guns n' Roses charting high on Billboard, not even like U2. One could argue that these bands were outside the mainstream and sounded nothing like Michael Jackson, Paula Abdul, or Michael Bolton, and of course, this is true. The difference though, is massive. Nirvana was completely and totally unknown. They didn't exist one minute and seemingly took over the world the next. U2 had already become huge after Live Aid in 1985 and was an early MTV staple. Metallica had been around since the early 80's but changed their look and sound so that radio and MTV would finally accept them. This happened in a big way with the release of *Metallica* (simply referred to as the Black Album) in August of 1991. In terms of Guns n' Roses, they hadn't been around as long as U2 or Metallica. Their now classic debut album, *Appetite for Destruction* was released on July 21st, 1987, and almost immediately made them the biggest band in the world for a while. So, it's no surprise that they too would be high on the Billboard charts come late 1991. Nirvana though? The band my friend Frank referred to as "Nevada". The band Pat included on this mixtape with other unknown bands from a few years ago was now about to become the biggest band in the world, and eventually one of the biggest and most important bands of all time. How? A band that would soon dethrone Michael Jackson from the top of the charts. What the hell is this sorcery anyway? As crazy as it sounds, this is exactly what took place.

Even with MTV soon adding "Smells Like Teen Spirit" to heavy rotation on all its shows, even in primetime, *Nevermind* didn't reach the number one spot on the Billboard charts until January 11, 1992. It was a quick ascension, but it wasn't overnight. When they did reach this milestone, however, they did it with a very significant and powerful move. If a band or musician wanted to slay the dragon as it were in the '80s or early '90s on a commercial and global level, they had to take on the biggest dragon of them all, the King of Pop himself, Michael Jackson. So, when *Nevermind* climbed to the number one spot on January 11, 1992, it knocked off Michael Jackson's *Danger-*

CHAPTER 7 - 1991: THE EXPLOSION

ous, officially marking the arrival of the biggest and most important musical movement since Beatlemania in the early and mid-'60s.

Once that happened, the floodgates burst open and a herd of bands from Seattle started taking over the American and global landscape. Pearl Jam, Soundgarden, and Alice in Chains were getting nearly as much attention as Nirvana, and this was just the beginning. Although the music of these bands didn't sound anything alike, the people who created it did dress and look alike. Marrying that with the fact that they all came from the same city, the media began marketing the "Seattle Sound" and "Grunge" as one, specific sound. This wasn't true and anyone with ears could understand that, but it's easier to sell one package than many, individual bands.

Using the city, the looks, and the fashion of these bands, a media firestorm was born and kids all over the world started dressing like Kurt Cobain, Eddie Vedder, Chris Cornell, and Layne Staley. This wasn a significant development because the music that was popular before grunge took off came with a very buttoned-up and fancy style attached to it. Lots of colors and sequence and polished shoes had been replaced with ripped jeans and shorts, leggings, flannel shirts, and Doc Martens. Looking back now, that was the change that seemed like it happened overnight more so than the music. Human beings are visual, and fashion has always played a role in culture and society so it should come as no surprise that the look of grunge, as much as the sound of grunge, was on sale and a windfall of cash was about to be available for all involved.

"It's strange for me to think that I am the age now that many of these people were when they were making the music that would inform some of my views and help me live my life. This music saved my life." These words are from 27-year-old Chris Celona, co-founder of the largest grunge account on Instagram, Grunge Bible. As I write this, the account currently has 537K followers with monster engagement numbers on every post.

I began interacting with Chris, who runs the site with friend and co-founder, Ethan Shalaway, a few years ago. Over time, and once I decided to write this book, I realized that I wanted Chris to be a part of it as he embodies what I've always known to be true about this music and its ability to influence generation after generation.

As is always the case when I run into people who did not witness the beginning or rise of the grunge and alternative movement in person, I asked Chris how he even found this music and why it affected him the way it did.

"I was 10 or 11 years old and listening to rock radio when I was in my mom's car, and I'd hear staples like 'Alive' or 'Black Hole Sun' and it was this slow burn every time I'd hear them. I was drawn to this music but at the time I couldn't understand why. I mean, I was born in 1996, and Kurt Cobain had already been dead for two years so more than a decade later, why was this music meaningful to me?"

Fast forwarding to our discussion about why Chris and Ethan decided to start the Grunge Bible and using it as a possible explanation as to why at 10 or 11 he was so profoundly influenced by this music Chris said, "We get comments on the account from 14 and 15-year-olds regularly and the draw the music has on them is the same draw it has on you, and the same draw it has on me."

A statement like that is something I've felt and believed in for a very long time, well over 40 years at this point. Sometimes music has a way of grabbing hold of you and simply never letting go. I assume that is a prerequisite if you're trying to create a new musical genre, a seismic cultural shift, and have decades of lasting power to influence countless millions of people. In the case of what was coming out of Seattle in the early '90s, I've always contended that it wasn't as much the sound of the music as it was the lyrics and the feeling/atmosphere they created together.

Chris and I discussed this during our interview and the emotions and feelings generated by this music and ultimately the reaction by those who fell

CHAPTER 7 – 1991: THE EXPLOSION

in love with it played a significant role in why he and Ethan started the page to begin with.

"When I got to college, I met the guy I would eventually run the account with. His name is Ethan Shalaway, and he's a drummer. We connected because we were both very passionate about music. As time went on, we started going to YouTube to watch grunge videos and for some reason started looking at the comments on each one. We found that all these people had really intense relationships with this music and wanted to learn why. We discovered the song 'Release' by Pearl Jam (off their 1991 debut album Ten) and there were hundreds upon hundreds of comments about how this song kept them alive. These types of songs just knock you over when you realize what they're about. After we saw all of this and felt the same way as these other people did, we knew we had to go all in. This was our path."

When people feel that type of connection with a certain kind of music, it's usually something that lasts a lifetime. Age, gender, socioeconomic status, geography, etc. means next to nothing when a lyric, guitar riff, passionate vocal, and rhythm hit you in all the right places. When Chris and I were speaking about this I mentioned that my 10-year-old daughter, who does like some of the music I play, listens to the contemporary music she's growing up with, like Taylor Swift, Billie Eilish, and Olivia Rodrigo. I told him about the time I brought up the fact that Rodrigo plays the 1994 hit song "Seether" by Veruca Salt during her live shows and how my daughter loved the original as much as Rodrigo's version. This is another great example of how the younger generation of fans and artists (Rodrigo is only 20 years old) are being influenced by grunge and alternative music released decades before they were even born. It was at this time that Chris shared with me that Rodrigo was an early follower of the Grunge Bible Instagram account.

"Olivia Rodrigo used to follow us before she stopped following anyone on social media. She was an original Grunge Bible fan," Chris said.

A very distinct memory I have of how quickly and easily the music of

ROB JANICKE

1991 penetrated my soul and revealed itself to me was on my walks on Saturday and Sunday mornings from my mom's house in Brooklyn to the local bowling alley where I worked throughout parts of high school and college. It was about a 10–12-minute walk or a five-minute drive but oftentimes, on nice days, I opted to walk so I could take advantage of the extra time and listen to my Walkman longer than I could by driving the five minutes and probably hear nothing but commercials on my way to work. Pearl Jam released its debut album Ten on August 27, 1991, to little fanfare. I had been somewhat in the know however because of the tape I've referenced throughout the book given to me by my friend Pat.

Green River was one of the bands on the tape and as I've also mentioned, they eventually evolved into Mudhoney and Mother Love Bone who then became Temple of the Dog, and ultimately, Pearl Jam. It's good to know people who know things most others don't. Pat was like my own personal internet before there was an internet. Back to the Walkman story. As I'd take these fifteen-minute walks in the late Summer/early Fall of '91 at 7 AM on the weekends, I would listen intently to the music and lyrics coming off Ten.

The songs "Alive" and "Release" both had a profound impact on me. I give the songwriting and musicianship of the band credit for sure, but it was the lyrics and especially the voice of Eddie Vedder that I connected with the most. A deep and gravelly baritone with purpose and emotion spilling out of my headphones, along with lyrics (from "Alive") describing personal strife related to his upbringing, particularly the inconceivable story about growing up with a man whom he believed to be his biological father and a seldom seen family friend who was, in fact, his biological father though not learning that truth until that man sadly passed away, sent chills up and down my spine every time I'd hear it.

As if that wasn't enough, the droning, melancholic sounds of "Release" accompanied by lyrics where Eddie is talking directly to his deceased father, begging to be released from the pain and confusion that has always plagued

CHAPTER 7 - 1991: THE EXPLOSION

him since learning the truth is nothing short of heart-wrenching. Especially if you have a complicated relationship with your dad as I've always had in my life. All of this, with the way the world and my life at 18 years old was, looking back now, was the clear reason why this music, from these people, Pearl Jam and the other bands of the era, was and is my music.

In addition to the music that was released in 1991, a very significant cultural event was born, mainly due to the burgeoning underground alternative music scene of the mid to late 1980s. Live music is perhaps the biggest part of any music experience. You can listen to all the albums you'd like, read all the biographies, and watch all the music documentaries but without seeing a band live and drowning in their vibe, you won't understand the music you're listening to. Even the best studio production in the world will not capture the essence of who and what an artist or a band is truly about. This concept was not lost in 1991, and the greatest example of this was the traveling music and arts festival, Lollapalooza.

Music festivals were nothing new, but Lollapalooza was very different in concept, creation, and execution. Inspired in part by festivals such as Britain's Reading Festival, Lollapalooza was the brainchild of Jane's Addiction's frontman Perry Farrell along with artist manager and entrepreneur Ted Gardner, music executives Don Muller and Marc Geiger as a farewell tour for Jane's Addiction.

The two biggest differences between Lollapalooza and other music festivals before or at that time were the fact that it was a traveling spectacle with side stages promoting lesser-known bands and the addition of booths and tents dedicated to art, politics, and culture. It was something the music world hadn't yet seen but was sorely needed. They couldn't have known this at the time, but Lollapalooza became a musical and cultural institution for the next 30 years and will likely continue for as long as music festivals exist.

Once again, the idea of age and timing played a tremendous role in my ability to witness this last great musical revolution firsthand. I was lucky enough to have attended the first three Lollapalooza tours. These shows were beyond transformative for me and the thousands of others like me who were in attendance.

If you weren't old enough or even alive in the early 90's it's hard for you to fully understand the impact that Lollapalooza had on not only the music scene but on culture. It was the 90's version of Woodstock, but in my opinion, was more important and had more of a lasting effect on the culture than Woodstock did. This take will certainly fire up a debate but I'm ready for it so maybe that's the next book!

As a quick aside, in 2007, as a freelance music writer, I was hired to cover the tour, which was now a stationary event held in Grant Park, Chicago for a magazine called, *Festival Preview*. It was one of those moments where your life comes full circle, and you see things from a brand-new perspective. For now, though, let's talk about the 90's lineups first, shall we?

In 1991, the inaugural Lollapalooza tour consisted of an eclectic lineup of bands and musicians who would shape the future of popular and underground music for decades to come. The influence these bands had on the global music scene cannot be underestimated.

On a hot summer afternoon, August 11, 1991, I witnessed one of the best experiences I had seen up until that point in my life. Butthole Surfers, Ice-T, Living Colour, Siouxie and the Banshees, Nine Inch Nails, Rollins Band, and Jane's Addiction laid the foundation for what was to be 30-plus years of incredible music, visual art, community, and cultural importance for Generation Xers the world over.

In addition to the musical and cultural significance, Lollapalooza became *our* thing. The '60s were over, the '70s were a blur, the indulgence and emotional bankruptcy of the '80s had become intolerable, so the '90s had an opportunity to rule the day . . . and the decade did not disappoint.

Every music scene has its markers. They all have their moments that define what they are. Be it Elvis on the Ed Sullivan Show, The Beatles landing

CHAPTER 7 - 1991: THE EXPLOSION

in America, Jimi Hendrix playing "The Star-Spangled Banner" at Woodstock, or Lollapalooza I, these moments are cemented in time and can, and never will be, forgotten. Some scenes, however, transcend music and become a part of or even create culture. Each generation, if they had a transcendent and culturally significant music scene attached to them will claim their scene was the best and most important in history. Of course, all of them cannot be right and so much of it is subjective anyway, but this will not stop people from declaring their scene as *the* scene. I do not blame them because I'm here to do the same for the early '90s.

Despite Lollapalooza's global success and obvious cultural significance, not everyone liked or appreciated the festival. One person, who also played a crucial role in the sound of some of the biggest alternative bands of the '90s, had some very harsh criticisms of Lollapalooza.

Famed record producer and audio engineer, Steve Albini, has worked with many of the biggest names in alternative music and because of that, has contributed to their massive success. His roster is a who's who of '90s giants like Nirvana, Pixies, PJ Harvey, The Breeders, Veruca Salt, and more. He's even worked with superstar veterans like Jimmy Page, Robert Plant, Cheap Trick, and others.

One would think that he'd like or at least appreciate something as special as Lollapalooza, yet this is what he's said about the festival in a 1993 interview found on Obselete.com with Jon Bains.

"Lollapalooza is the worst example of corporate encroachment into what is supposed to be the underground. It is just a large-scale marketing of bands that pretend to be alternative but are in reality just another facet of the mass cultural exploitation scheme. I have no appreciation or affection for those bands, and I have no interest in that whole circle. If Lollapalooza had Jesus Lizard and the Melvins and Fugazi and Slint then you could make a case that it was actually people on the vanguard of music. What it really is the most popular bands on MTV that are not heavy metal."

Everyone is entitled to their opinion and Albini certainly has enough credibility through his work that he should be heard, but this take seems a bit hypocritical to me since he's partially responsible for the bands he's engineered and/or produced successes. In the case of the early Lollapalooza line-ups, especially the first one, it would be a huge stretch to say that bands such as Butthole Surfers, Rollins Band, or Siouxie and the Banshees were some of the most popular bands on MTV or commercial radio in 1991 so Steve would be off base a little bit here.

There's always been a fine line, and in a way, a made-up line, between commercial and underground music. Most bands begin in the underground by the sheer fact that no one knows who they are. Some like to remain that way even after achieving some success. A great example of this is the legendary hardcore band out of Washington, D.C., Fugazi.

Fugazi was started by Minor Threat frontman Ian MacKaye. Minor Threat was pivotal in the hardcore punk scene and their influence can still be heard today in various genres including punk, post-punk, emo, and of course, hardcore music. MacKaye is also the co-founder and owner of the independent record label, Dischord Records. His influence and importance on the rock music scene in the late '80s/early '90s cannot be overstated.

After gaining a cult following with Minor Threat, MacKaye, along with Guy Picciotto, Joe Lally, and Brendan Canty formed Fugazi in 1986. You would be hard-pressed to find a band that emerged from the '90s, with even a remote connection to punk rock, who wasn't inspired by Fugazi. Fugazi masterfully straddled the line between underground and commercial success. They were known to everyone in the scene, played all over the world, released incredible records, and did make money, but never fully crossed over into the mainstream.

Not every band can operate on the margins like Fugazi did and not everyone can function in the mainstream like Jane's Addiction or later, Pearl Jam was able to. Music is not an exact science and there aren't many rules to

CHAPTER 7 - 1991: THE EXPLOSION

follow. It's rebellious by nature and artists aren't used to being told what to do or how to follow rules anyway. That's why they're artists and not accountants. So, for Albini to levy that type of harsh criticism onto mainstream bands or "commercial" festivals like Lollapalooza seems a bit disingenuous.

Regardless of who says what's good or bad regarding Lollapalooza, there's enough evidence out there for me to believe that its very creation, and execution, at least in its first few years, was essential in developing the Gen X legacy from a music and culture perspective.

1991 is the year most music and cultural historians point to when discussing the grunge and alternative movement because it was the year that *Nevermind* was released, and seeing as how Kurt Cobain and Nirvana became the most recognizable symbol of the era, it makes sense. With crossover albums such as Pearl Jam's *Ten* (released in August), Soundgarden's *Badmotorfinger* (released in October), and *Nevermind* (released in September), all coming out toward the end of '91 and needing about four to six months to take off, one could argue that 1992-1997 were the years that truly cemented the legacy of the era for decades to come.

It's important to remember what I touched upon earlier regarding timing. There's an entire world that operates outside the spectrum of music. Governments, religions, educational systems, and so forth, all, for the most part, operate outside the world of music. Music, for many people, is nothing more than an escape. It keeps people company on their commutes to and from work or school, helps them relax and sleep at night, and allows them to let off steam while dancing or working out. Something major happens though, when instead of assisting with the activities of daily life, it becomes daily life. It happened in the 1960s and it happened again in the 1990s.

Music became the conversation and the catalyst for a generational shift in global thought. It was a force behind social, cultural, and eventually, political change. This was only possible because the climate in the '60s, and again in the '90s, had dictated change was needed. I think it was more urgent and obvious in the '60s and more underground and nefarious in the '90s, but either way, change was destined to happen. That's the thing about music, it has power and reach beyond most, if not all, mediums and art forms. Something happens to your physiology and brain chemistry when listening to music. There are so many studies and essays on the subject because the scientific community agrees on how powerful music is. Consider the assertion of Stefan Koelsch, Professor of Biological Psychology, Medical Psychology, and Music Psychology at the University of Bergen (Norway):

"Music is capable of evoking exceptionally strong emotions and of reliably affecting the mood of individuals. Functional neuroimaging and lesion studies show that music-evoked emotions can modulate activity in virtually all limbic and paralimbic brain structures. These structures are crucially involved in the initiation, generation, detection, maintenance, regulation and termination of emotions that have survival value for the individual and the species. Therefore, at least some music-evoked emotions involve the very core of evolutionarily adaptive neuroaffective mechanisms. Because dysfunctions in these structures are related to emotional disorders, a better understanding of music-evoked emotions and their neural correlates can lead

to a more systematic and effective use of music in therapy." (Trends in Cognitive Sciences 2010)

You do not need to take a tremendous leap of faith to understand the known implications, as well as the importance that music carries for the entirety of the human species. All art forms are critical for human interaction, expression, and education. Music, however, is the ringleader. I'm reminded of John Lennon's brilliant song "Imagine" and the global impact it had from the time of its release in 1971 through this exact moment in time today. Lennon was able to, in just over three minutes, describe so succinctly, a world in which the great majority of people would like to live in. It's probably the most straightforward plea for a peaceful existence in any song ever written. The

CHAPTER 7 - 1991: THE EXPLOSION

effect it had is something described in books, magazines, and films thousands of times over.

In 2017, the National Music Publishers Association awarded "Imagine" the Centennial Song Award, anointing the track the most influential song of the past 100 years. It is a once-in -a-lifetime song in terms of its reach and influence. Passionate music, however, played to people who are in the middle of an existence they're unhappy with is more powerful than some people are willing to admit. Those who see it though, those who've experienced its power and its ability to affect change, hold music as close to their hearts and souls as anything else they couldn't live without. This is what was brewing, what was boiling in the late 1980s and exploded all over the globe in the early 1990s. A new generation of kids who were confused, angry, and apathetic about everything from their home lives, their schools, their government, and their future (or lack thereof) was the perfect audience and eventually cultural warriors who would take the explosion started by Nirvana and stoke those flames for the next 30 years.

CHAPTER 8 – 1992-1993
THIS IS DANGEROUS: THE ANGST GOT ANGSTIER

"THEY JUST BLEW UP THE WORLD TRADE CENTER," A FRIEND YELLED OUT. "WHAT? WHAT ARE you talking about, that's impossible," I said. "It's on the news!!" he yelled louder.

It was 1993 and I was a few months shy of my twentieth birthday when I learned what so much of the world and kids my age and younger had known, terrorism. In a post-9/11 world, what I just wrote wouldn't be that shocking to a 19-year-old in 2024 because they'd unfortunately be well-versed in bombings, terrorist plots, and mass executions the world over. These are the times we live in now. In 1993, however, this was science fiction come to life.

On February 26, 1991, a massive explosion occurred in the parking garage underneath the World Trade Center in New York City killing 6 people and injuring over 1,000 more. This was the moment most New Yorkers, and Americans for that matter, grew up. Our comfort and safety had been shaken to its core and the way we looked at the world would be changed forever. Already battling internal demons for most of my life, the anxiety and fear this event caused now turned those demons toward the outside world as well.

With Nirvana knocking Michael Jackson out of the number one spot on the Billboard charts by mid-January 1992, the world was now officially aware of and pre-warned about the sonic deluge that was about to wash over the planet for the next few years. Grunge and alternative music, fashion, punk rock idealism, and marketing, had been given the green light by the massive success of *Nevermind*, to begin its relentless takeover of popular culture.

Musically speaking, 1992 was a continuation of what had been released the year prior in terms of pushing the envelope further with music from Seattle and now, other towns and cities looking to export their scene to the masses. One would think that the creation of a "scene," specifically when it's centered around music and culture, would take a while to get into all the nooks and crannies of society and make irrelevant what was there before. In the case of the grunge or Seattle Scene, the takeover was instantaneous.

On November 26, 1991, international superstar, the "King of Pop," Michael Jackson, released his eighth studio album, *Dangerous* via Epic Records. It debuted at number one on the Billboard Top 200 Albums chart and went on to sell over 32 million copies since its release. It remained at the top spot on the charts for four consecutive weeks. Its main competition was Country music crossover sensation Garth Brooks with his album, *Ropin' The Wind*. The country was being run, musically speaking, by what was perhaps the definition of Pop music in Michael Jackson, and a radio-friendly, watered-down version of country music, in the form of Garth Brooks. Not exactly revolution-stirring, flip-your-soul-upside-down, generation-defining music. This fact makes what happened next even more shocking. It's rare after essentially being lulled to sleep for years by anything, including boring music, to suddenly be awoken by a volcanic eruption.

For those who were paying attention, this day was coming. It was creeping and sneaking its way into America's cultural consciousness, but the mainstream wasn't paying much attention. Sure, you had the "underground," every generation had its version. That part of society is usually reserved for people who can't be bothered with what's going on "above ground" and they're happy to live in quiet rebellion beneath the corporate mockery walking around just

CHAPTER 8 – 1992-1993: THIS IS DANGEROUS

above their heads. In early 1992, however, those dwelling just beneath the surface were on a collision course with the young and mainly silent group of kids who were about to define the next musical revolution.

When Billboard released its Top 200 chart for the week of January 11th, 1992, the revolution was officially announced. This is the week in which Nirvana's *Nevermind* overtook the albums by both Michael Jackson and Garth Brooks as the number-one album in the country. As you read this now it probably doesn't sound very startling. At this point, all three of the artists just mentioned are legendary, household names who we know almost everything about. You must believe me when I tell you though, for this to have happened in 1992, however, it was as unpredictable as anything could be on a commercial level. This is one of the reasons I was compelled to write this book. The magnitude of what took place on the charts, radio, and MTV was simply through the roof. Music, culture, fashion, lexicon, social causes, politics, and life as we knew it, especially for high school and college-aged kids, was forever changed. It wasn't just pop music that was wiped away. Even versions of rock music felt the wrath of grunge. No one was immune. Genres like heavy metal, more specifically, "hair metal," the lighter, friendlier, made-for-MTV version of metal, took a massive blow.

"I worked at MTV back in those days, so I really saw it coming," says comedian and co-host of *That Metal Show*, Don Jamieson, when I interviewed him for this book. "But at the same time, some of those bands were really great. Bands like Soundgarden and Alice in Chains were very Sabbath-like so you couldn't help but like them."

As I said before, the grunge movement displaced a lot of hard rock and heavy metal bands, mainly a subgenre of metal commonly referred to as "hair metal." Bands like Motley Crue, Poison, Warrant, and Bon Jovi were at the top of their game and the radio and MTV charts in the mid and late '80s and didn't see the tsunami of drop D-tuned guitars and messages of isolation and alienation coming straight at them. It cannot be stressed enough that when grunge hit, it truly was like a left hook coming out of nowhere. There were plenty of lead-up and warning signs in the underground as I've been alluding to but the mainstream music industry, with all its pomp, circumstance, and God complexes abound, felt invincible. Honestly, who could blame them? When the number one song on the Billboard Year-End Hot 100 Singles of 1990 chart was "Hold On" by Wilson Phillips, where was the threat exactly? With Jon Bon Jovi and Billy Idol, the heaviest (if my keyboard had a smirk key, I'd use it here) acts in the top ten of that same list, what could the record label executives possibly fear?

"Metal was not dangerous anymore," proclaimed Jamieson. "It had become predictable in so many ways, it became a parody of itself and grunge and alternative was going in a different direction." Even before 1991, fans of heavy music, at least those with their ears partially attached to the underground, knew something different, something cooler was brewing.

"I loved Jane's Addiction when they first came out because they were dangerous," admits Jamieson, a lifelong metal fan who is very loyal to the bands he grew up loving. "The danger element of Jane's is what attracted me to them, and I think that's also why a band like Guns N' Roses survived the '90s because they too were dangerous."

Through 2015, *Nevermind* spent 477 weeks on the Billboard 200 Albums chart. That was good enough for 9th all-time. (Billboard Magazine 2015). Again, through the lens of hindsight, this all makes perfect sense. At the start of the initial takeover, it was unfathomable. It just couldn't happen, except it did. They say the eye of the hurricane is where it's most calm during the violence of any storm. Being in that eye as this all unfolded, it wasn't easy to see how significant it was, though we knew something was happening.

Even as kids we understood that taking down the "King of Pop" in any musical category and making pop music virtually irrelevant for a few years was cool. Looking back now though and realizing nothing like that has even come close to happening again, is beyond monumental. Time is a slow but re-

CHAPTER 8 - 1992-1993: THIS IS DANGEROUS

lentless teacher. It affords us the ability to question and think, remember, and reconcile all that we've gone through. Life changes daily and when you think about how many days make up thirty years, that's a ton of change. Nothing can be stagnant while living on a planet that's in constant motion. With the hindsight of 10,950 days (thirty years), you can damn well bet your life has changed thousands of times over. One constant for me, and millions like me, is the music that started the change in the first place. The importance of that cannot be overstated. It's as much a part of who we were and who we became as anything else in our lives and thus should be treated with great reverence.

As 1992 plowed forward, it became abundantly clear that I had found my "tribe." Not only had Nirvana taken over the world, but other bands from Seattle, all with roots older than theirs, came into prominence. Pearl Jam was the sum of the parts from Seattle pioneers Green River and then Mother Love Bone. Soundgarden had been around since 1984, Alice In Chains formed in 1987, and dozens of others from the region had now become mainstays on radio, the national touring circuit, and MTV. For many reasons, Kurt's untimely death being the biggest one, Nirvana didn't last very long. As a matter of fact, out of the four bands mentioned, Pearl Jam is the only one still intact with its core lineup. Alice In Chains is still around and making very good music but their lead singer and face of the band, Layne Staley, died after a very long battle with drug addiction on April 5 (same date as Cobain strangely enough), 2002. The band took some time and eventually reemerged with a new lead singer, William DuVall in 2006.

As for Soundgarden, they initially called it quits in 1997. In 2001, lead singer Chris Cornell joined forces with the members of another early 90's mega-band, Rage Against the Machine (minus singer Zack de la Rocha) to form the formidable Audioslave. After some critical and commercial success (over 8 million records sold in 6 years), Audioslave broke up in 2007. A few years later, in 2010, Cornell reunited with Soundgarden for the second phase of that band's career. Sadly though, on May 18th, 2017, Chris Cornell committed suicide by hanging himself in a Detroit hotel room after a Soundgarden performance earlier that night.

What happened in the early 90's, beginning in Seattle, Washington, and making its way around the globe over these past thirty years, has tentacles reaching all aspects of the complexities that make up human life. The stories, accounts, and lessons that emerged from this dynamic moment in time have affected so much more than the music it created. Music has proven scientific effects on our brains when we listen. Beyond that, it helps create a psychological profile of not only who we are as listeners, but who we become as people. I've dedicated many pages in this book to that end. I know for myself, as well as so many others, that what transpired during those early days of the 1990s, listening to the music and the messaging coming from it all, helped to create a generation of thought, and eventually action, which we took and implemented for the rest of our lives.

The fuse to the new musical future was lit in the Fall of 1991 and the fires from that initial explosion began to erupt everywhere. Most of those fires became explosions, some louder than others of course, but all explosions, nonetheless. *Nevermind* was the trailblazer, the boot that kicked the door open to the mainstream. Nirvana though, in comparison to the three Seattle bands mentioned a few moments ago, wasn't the first band to form. That distinction belongs to Soundgarden whose history dates to 1984. The founders of Pearl Jam, Stone Gossard and Jeff Ament, were in Green River dating back to '84 as well. They would go on to form Mother Love Bone in 1988 and release that band's debut album (*Apple*) more than a year before *Nevermind* was released. Alice in Chains was formed in 1987 (like Nirvana) but released their first album, *Facelift* in August of 1990. The list of bands from the Seattle area, who would go on to become quite popular throughout the '90s, who either formed before Nirvana or released their debut album before *Nevermind* came out is long. It's almost impossible to imagine that any of these bands would have become known outside of the Pacific Northwest, let alone become some

CHAPTER 8 - 1992-1993: THIS IS DANGEROUS

of the biggest bands in music history, without Nirvana's *Nevermind*. I'm certain it wouldn't have happened.

Some names you should recognize are: Screaming Trees, Melvins, Tad, Babes in Toyland, and Mudhoney. Mudhoney formed when Green River broke up and essentially turned into two bands, the other being Mother Love Bone and eventually Pearl Jam. Like in any local scene, so many of the players, at least at the start, were intertwined with each other. If you've ever been in a band or around bands in a thriving, local music scene, you know how often they share players, break up and form new bands, play in more than one at a time, etc. It's part of the fabric that makes a scene possible. There is inherent competition but there's also a comradery that comes along with a local music scene.

The smart people know that if one band "makes it" then the light will be shining on their town and others will have a chance to be heard by people never thought possible. Perhaps there's always a battle for which band will break through first, egos can be quite large in bands at times, but it's usually good for the entire scene if any one of them becomes big. Seattle in the late '80s and early '90s was no different.

The bands in Seattle had help though. It's certainly romantic to think that a few friends got together in a garage, practiced every day for months, recorded a demo, sent it off to a major label, and "voila," became the biggest band in the world. It pretty much never happens like that, and it didn't happen with Nirvana in Seattle either. A local scene, especially one that becomes so big it takes over the world, needs more than just great musicians. It needs people who believe in those great musicians, will promote those musicians, and put out their records. Even with all of that in place, most scenes die out without anyone knowing they existed outside a 10-mile radius of their hometown. The odds of making it onto the radio are tough enough, let alone having anyone in other cities or states even know your name. It's a bit different now in the digital age but still nearly impossible to make it big. Can you imagine how difficult it was in the mid and late '80s? If you were in a band and you had a song on your local college radio station, that would likely be your highest-ranking musical achievement ever.

Location also had a lot to do with success back then. If you were in New York, Los Angeles, Chicago, or London you had somewhat of a chance because the media and the world at large paid attention to cities like those. But Seattle? No way. In 1991, most people probably couldn't point to it on a map if asked. The hurdles this music scene had to jump over to do what it did were beyond astronomical. Perhaps that's why it was 30 years in the making since the last big scene in the 1960s. It's damn hard to do.

If you've seen any documentaries, read any books, or even spoken with anyone from the Seattle scene, you've likely heard the term "The year punk broke" about 1991. This is one of those situations when several things can be true at one time. In my opinion that statement is both true and false all at once. Simply put, "punk" broke (again) in 1991 on a commercial level. If left at that, the statement can be true. The problem is nothing becomes a commercial success without a massive audience.

In the case of Seattle in 1991, the massive audience that was seemingly born of Nirvana's release of *Nevermind* did not come out of thin air. It was an audience being built and cultivated for at least 10 years prior from the punk and hardcore underground scene. Remember that infamous tape I discussed given to me by my friend Pat? That tape, which did have a Nirvana track ("About a Girl" from *Bleach*) on it, also had bands and musicians from the early and mid-'80s on it who came with their own passionate and dedicated fan bases. To understand Nirvana's success, as with almost everything in life, you need to understand not only the conditions of the day but all that came before it as well. Punk music "broke" in the '70s and you can't break something twice. So that statement from earlier in the paragraph has inherent flaws as you can see. I've even heard people say that 1991 was the revival of punk music. Maybe that's more accurate than saying it broke but I guess the

CHAPTER 8 – 1992-1993: THIS IS DANGEROUS

point here is that punk rock never went away. Just because the masses don't know about it or accept it, doesn't mean it doesn't exist. Nirvana had the massive success it had, in large part, because they were fans of so many of the punk and hardcore punk bands who came before them and knew others were possibly ready to take it to the next level. Regardless, they knew the fans were there because they were a part of that same fan base their entire lives.

One of the elements that always remains true when it comes to any cultural movement is that it's reactionary. Something is happening within the societal norm and a faction of the population, usually the youth, rises and rejects it. It's human nature, a rite of passage if you will. This happens for individuals and groups alike. Some of this rebellion is created out of boredom, and some of it is created out of necessity. The backlash doesn't always amount to a global takeover, however. Most often it's an annoying buzz in the ear of those who discount everything anyway so what's the point? Maybe it satisfies the teen angst and "fuck off" attitude that comes with being a kid who sees the world as nothing more than a black hole and is trying like hell not to get sucked in.

Occasionally, though, the angst is powerful enough, the black hole scary enough, and the powers that be complacent enough for a perfect storm of rebellion to thrive. Many things seem to call people to action and give them the fuel they need to stand up for what they believe in. You can never tell just what the impetus is going to be from person to person but once they move, they typically won't stop until their voices are heard and their changes made. It's a gamble and a duty all at the same time. There aren't any guarantees and sometimes, depending on who the fight is against, you can open yourself up to physical harm. Every position taken has someone or something on the other side waiting to knock it down. The fall may be painful, but it seldom deters those hard-charging for their truth.

Make no mistake though, culture and counterculture, rebellion and authority, us against them, and all the descriptions one can use to explore these movements, are here to stay. It's built into our fabric as people and societies, it's just who we are. Look no further than the debut releases of Tool *Opiate* and the self-titled *Rage Against The Machine*, and you can't help but feel the anger blasting through the speakers. Whether it's organized religion and authority or national and international governments, war, and oppression, the topics being discussed are heavy, in your face, unapologetic, and angry. Commercial music was certainly taking a turn toward angst and there was little anyone could do to stop it. More on both bands in a little bit.

Looking back thirty years and seeing everything that transpired in 1991, culminating with the release of *Nevermind* has brought so much back into focus. Not that I'd ever lost focus to begin with per se, but three decades is a very long time. Many of the lessons I learned and stances I took have remained by my side like a long shadow on a sunny day since those very early days. Thinking back to those times, through all the various lenses I've picked up throughout the years does shine a light on many aspects of what and why things went down the way they did. Writing this book helps me make sense of what was and what became, in ways I hadn't completely understood until putting words on a page. It was rebellious and it was counterculture. It was a reaction to and a striking down of, the world kids in their late teens and early twenties were living in. It was easy enough though to perhaps leave it at that in terms of a reason and then just stage dive into the pit and get through each day just to listen to another CD or go to another show.

With all this hindsight now though, it's easier to understand the truly massive and important effect it had on the people who surfed its first wave. I'd like to think I would've become the person I am now without the aid of a once-in-a-lifetime musical revolution but I'm not that naive. I'm being reminded more so now than ever before that I have a strong and direct link to the music scene I was lucky enough to enter adulthood with. The sounds, the words, the sights, the perceptions, and attitudes all had varying but important roles in shaping who I am today. Later in the book, you'll meet other people

CHAPTER 8 - 1992-1993: THIS IS DANGEROUS

who acknowledge this for themselves as well. I've talked with people who were also genuinely affected even though they were either too young to have witnessed it firsthand or were already embedded in careers and/or families during the early '90s yet feel and realize its importance in their lives.

What is it about music that would compel famed philosopher Friedrich Nietzsche to say, "Without music, life would be a mistake?"

People like Nietzsche, as well as scientists, psychologists, and other renowned thinkers, have said similar things throughout history. What is it about musical notes, chords, melodies, and the sound of a human voice that can bring people to their knees? Create emotion so palpable that the body runs through its machinations to cause tiny hairs to stand at attention, skin to become rife with goose bumps, or tears to fall from the eyes? Why and how is this possible? There are theories backed by decades of research and analysis from great minds who've dedicated their lives to figuring this out. I explore some of these throughout the book and I hope we shed some light on this phenomenon.

As much as I respect science and dedicated research, there is an answer to why and how music does what it does that's as acceptable as any I suppose. That answer is "Who knows, but I can't live without it," and you know, sometimes that's all that matters. After all, music *is* about emotion, and we care about how it makes us feel so occasionally, I can live with this response. Who knows if all the science and analysis in the world can give us a better answer, even if we're ok with the easy answer of "who knows, but I can't live without it," it's too important a topic to leave alone. We can get and do have scientific answers to these wonderful questions, and they need to be explored. It's part of the human condition, it's another step in trying to understand what we are as a species. It's an exercise in self-knowledge, growth, evolution.

These are questions I don't believe I was asking myself back in 1991. I'm pretty sure others weren't either, not directly anyway. What I (and the rest of that generation) was asking was why someone who felt out of place within his own family and circle of friends finds acceptance and comfort in music made by people we didn't know in places we'd possibly never see. This question, and others like it, had started for me around 1985 or 1986. I was 13 or 14 years old and the world I was trying to fit into was not only becoming less interesting, but it also just wasn't making any sense. I come from a divorced home, raised by a mother who was always working two, sometimes three jobs, just to keep a roof over our heads. I have a younger sister whom I was tasked to look after even though we're not even two full years apart, so I had to grow up quickly. I'm also a product of Catholic school as I mentioned earlier, and those teachings made absolutely no sense to me. So, I was witness to a broken home, was a latchkey kid, saw right through religion, and had no desire to adhere to or duplicate any of it. The music I was listening to at that time was good (classic rock and heavy metal), but I couldn't fully relate to the messages in them. I was either too young or just not interested in some of the topics these songs were putting out there.

Then, almost out of nowhere, I discovered punk rock, rap, and what would eventually be dubbed alternative and grunge music. This was the start of what would prove to be a life-long love affair with meaningful, thought-provoking, emotionally driven music. I became obsessed. I read all the magazines (no internet in the '80s remember) and books I could get my hands on. I studied lyrics and liner notes printed in albums and cassettes. I tried talking adults into taking me to concerts I was too young to attend alone. I knew what this music FELT like, and I was fine with not knowing more about why I felt it. The bigger, more complex questions came later. This period was all about discovery, knowledge, and an unquenchable thirst for more.

In 1992, just as Nirvana was topping the charts, people like me were starting to get some answers, whether we realized it or not, to the questions we started asking ourselves five or so years earlier. By the time *Nevermind* hit number one, I was in the second semester of my freshman year of college. There's an interesting parallel to being in a scholastic environment such as

CHAPTER 8 - 1992-1993: THIS IS DANGEROUS

a university and beginning to understand something very powerful about yourself that has absolutely nothing to do with school.

Although science agrees that our personalities develop as children, I can say that my understanding of culture formed in real-time during the early '90s. My already formed personality was now being introduced to a way of life I was enthralled with. How would the two mesh? Would my younger self accept these new and potent times? Was I going to subject myself to this chaotic, culture shock of a lifestyle or was I going to hold firm to teachings from my past which I had already dismissed as bogus? The dilemma of pleasing others or being completely true to yourself is something that, 30 years later, I struggle with daily. Music though, is what drives me, and millions of others, to continue to search for the courage to do what you know is right. Although these are everyday struggles that many people have, the music of the early '90s did focus on the inner turmoil that many kids of the day felt. Let's face it, the artists making this music weren't much older than me at the time. Most of the bands from Seattle which made all the commercial noise at first were made up of people in their mid-20s. They were feeling the same things as they were listening to underground bands such as Black Flag, Minor Threat, Dead Kennedys, Bad Brains, and others. They were carrying the torch lit for them years ago and we were the recipients of its heat. This was a calling as well as a call-out. The rest of our lives were developing before our very eyes with their music filling our ears and our souls.

Seattle still reigned supreme (and would for a few more years) but since the music industry has always been a copycat business, record labels were quick to sign anyone with long hair, flannel shirts, dark lyrics, and attitude to spare. By no means did this indicate that most of these bands didn't deserve to be heard or benefit from large record deals, many of them certainly did. As the decade marched on, however, we then saw the watering down of the initial burst of talent, angst, and despair.

One of the cities not named Seattle that jumped into the fray that was this new and extremely fast-growing genre was Los Angeles, California. No stranger to the limelight when it comes to entertainment, California has always been a breeding ground for some of the biggest names in the music industry. From Etta James to Dr. Dre, The Byrds to Guns N' Roses, The Eagles to Metallica, and so on. Los Angeles was never denied its spot in creating and shaping culture with its musical output and 1992 was no different. Many books have been written about the numerous bands and artists from this town and many more will someday come out as well. Truth be told, it's a topic unto itself as far as I'm concerned. When it comes to the commercial breakthrough of grunge and alternative music in 1992 however, I feel two bands shine above the rest. While strikingly different in sound and style, Tool and Rage Against the More Machine were as important as any band coming out of Seattle in terms of impact, messaging, and cultural shifts, and their lasting power to this very day is proof of this.

Formed in Los Angeles in 1990 by vocalist Maynard James Keenan, guitarist Adam Jones, drummer Danny Carey, and bassist Paul D'Amour (replaced in 1995 by Justin Chancellor), Tool had their take on what the '90s "Seattle sound" would be all about. Unlike the punk and '70s rock-influenced music of Nirvana and Pearl Jam respectively or the hard rock/psychedelic sound of Soundgarden, Tool was more along the lines of Alice In Chains as both share heavy metal leanings with a dark and sinister atmosphere. At a time when kids in the early '90s were looking for something to match the fear and loneliness they were feeling, Tool provided the perfect soundtrack to those ever-present emotions.

Be it the hushed and ominous whispers or the blood-curdling screams of Keenan's vocals or the aggressive picked tones of Tool's signature bass sound, this band spoke to millions of scared and disillusioned kids the world over. Their first, non-demo effort, an EP titled Opiate, was released by Zoo Records on March 10, 1992. The seven-track recording (the last song is hidden)

CHAPTER 8 - 1992-1993: THIS IS DANGEROUS

contains two live songs which was normal for a young band to release, especially on an EP. Containing some of the band's heaviest songs to date (later records would feature more groove-laden and prog-style metal), Opiate's lyrical content, mainly censorship and anti-religion messaging, would become the norm for future Tool albums. It was exactly what many in the new generation of music fans would need, even if they didn't know it at the time.

Not to be outdone in the musical significance department, another prominent early '90s band would explode out of L.A. and release a massively impactful record in 1992. Rage Against the Machine released its self-titled, debut album via Epic Records on November 3, 1992. The release, co-produced by the band, would prove to be the beginning of a new sub-genre, rap metal, which would be one of the most influential sounds of the decade and beyond. Vocalist Zack de la Rocha, guitarist Tom Morello, bassist Tim Commerford, and drummer Brad Wilk formed in Los Angeles in 1991 with the idea of merging two very different styles of music, heavy metal and rap, with punk rock attitude and protest lyrical content. The bold combination was a huge success as the band received critical and commercial acclaim, sold millions of albums, and eventually was inducted into the Rock 'n' Roll Hall of Fame in 2023.

Protest music has always had its place in society ever since there was a society to speak of. In the United States, protest songs can be traced as far back as the lead-up to the American Revolution. Dr. Joseph Warren, one of the earliest and most dedicated resistors toward the British tyranny of the American Colonies, wrote a song called "Free Americay" in 1774. This song was a direct response to the British government releasing the Intolerable Acts as punishment for the Boston Tea Party. Regardless of where they're from or what century they live or have lived in, people have an inherent desire for freedom and fairness. When these desires are infringed upon, some people act by taking stances against what oppresses them. Art has always existed to serve this purpose and music, being the loudest of the art forms, has always lent itself to people with a message of hope, fairness, opposition, and yes, freedom. Rage Against the Machine harnessed its message and delivered its version of pummeling protest music to the masses and has yet to relent.

I was fortunate enough to have seen both Tool and RATM early on in their existence and have been a fan of both bands ever since. As noted earlier in the book, I was a metalhead as a young child so Tool's ode to Black Sabbath and Rage's killer riffs and angst-laden vocals spoke to me in a language that felt like home. Along with what I was hearing and feeling out of Seattle, the early '90s were shaping up for me, and as the world would soon find out, hundreds of millions of others, as the greatest time in the history of music.

With new music and more importantly, new genres changing cultures and shaping generations, whatever existed before must fall. In the rock world, a cleaner, more radio-friendly version of heavy metal and hard rock ruled the radio and MTV airways in the late '80s and early '90s. By 1992 however, it was quite evident that a seismic change in the power structure had taken place. This left many music fans feeling less than thrilled about what was happening on their television screens and blasting through their radio speakers.

"I'm very loyal to the bands I grew up with, so 9 times out of 10 I go back to those cornerstone bands,'" said Don Jamieson. "I did take it personally that these new bands were knocking the crap out of my bands. Grunge came in like punk did in the '70s and it just wiped the slate clean. Grunge is our generation's punk rock," continued Jamieson.

I agree with that assessment because weirdly, part of me also felt a bit sad that things had changed so much in such a short period. This is the beauty of music though, as we all consume it and feel it based on where we are in our personal lives at the time, and for me, I guess I was more in need of a change than I had realized. Others weren't and that's fine. We're all on our journeys and need to follow what moves us so we wind up at the correct destination, wherever and whenever that may be.

Just like the year prior, 1992 was chock full of important releases span-

CHAPTER 8 - 1992-1993: THIS IS DANGEROUS

ning the grunge, alternative, and hip-hop landscape. These genres were only just beginning to find their footing and '92 played a big role in establishing new sounds that were creating a new culture. In discussing Tool and Rage Against the Machine, I wanted to highlight a couple of bands not from Seattle to show how the music scene was starting to spread outside of the Emerald City.

That being said, 1991 was still the year of Seattle, and one of the biggest and most influential bands from that town was Alice In Chains. They had been around since 1987 and as mentioned in the 1988-1990 chapter, released their debut album, *Facelift* in 1990, missing inclusion in the barrage of releases to come out just one year later. Beginning in late 1992, however, Alice In Chains would forever be included in all grunge-related conversations from here to eternity.

Released by Columbia Records on September 29, 1992, *Dirt* was the second studio album by Alice In Chains. Like *Facelift* before it, *Dirt* was produced by Dave Jerden (Frank Zappa, Jane's Addiction, Red Hot Chili Peppers, Meat Puppets, etc.) and would go on to become the band's best-selling release of its career. Before getting into *Dirt* though, a very quiet and surprising release happened several months prior.

Sap, an EP released on February 4, 1992, seemingly came out of nowhere after AIC had wrapped up its tour in support of *Facelift*. The band hadn't intended on writing or releasing an EP at this time and had only entered the studio to record a song for director Cameron Crowe's "(Fast Times at Ridgemont High", "Say Anything" . . . "Jerry Maguire", "Almost Famous", etc.) film roughly based on the burgeoning Seattle music scene, "Singles". The track, "Would?" became the song to wind up on the movie soundtrack but while in the studio the band took advantage of the time and the creative juices that were left over from just getting off tour. Alice In Chains would record around 10 songs which included everything that made up *Sap* and a few tracks that would find their way onto *Dirt*.

The late Rick Parashar, who died from complications of a pulmonary embolism in 2014 at the age of 50, mixed and produced this session, and his recording of "Would?" wound up on both *Singles* and *Dirt* and is the only track on *Dirt* not produced by Dave Jerden. If Rick Parashar sounds familiar, he should. In addition to the song "Would?" and the EP *Sap* for AIC, Parashar also produced hit albums, *Ten* (Pearl Jam), the self-titled *Temple of the Dog*, and the debut album by *Blind Melon* (also self-titled), among others.

The release of *Sap* at this time was a game-changer in many ways when it came to the expectations and what was "allowed" to be considered grunge. I know this sounds like there were some silly rules to follow but as I mentioned earlier, music did (and in some cases still does) have weird, made-up regulations by fans and critics as to what can be labeled as this or that. Most of us are guilty of these sophomoric tendencies, (I know I've had my moments) and my only hope is we can evolve past this insignificant labeling. Grunge was starting to be pigeonholed as loud, heavy, and sludgy-sounding rock but *Sap* changed all of that in an instant.

Sap was dark, but that's because of the vocals, melodies, and atmosphere created by the musical arrangements. What *Sap* wasn't was loud and electric. For a band like Alice In Chains to release an acoustic EP after the heavy riffing of *Facelift* (not to mention what they would be known for just a few months later with *Dirt)* was a bold move that should not be overlooked. This release not only expanded the sound of what grunge or alternative rock could be, but it also lent credence to the notion that this new music emanating from the Pacific Northwest felt like a private music club made by friends and membership was now available to the rest of us.

Looking back at those times, I got the feeling from the music and the interviews given by those making it, that it was an all-inclusive project. Anyone could do anything, and it was going to turn out to be something great. It didn't feel competitive like popular music had before Seattle started this new thing. *Sap* boasted guest musicians from Seattle all over the record. Ann

CHAPTER 8 - 1992-1993: THIS IS DANGEROUS

Wilson of the historic band Heart sang on the tracks "Brother" and "Am I Inside," and the song "Right Turn" is credited to the fictitious band dubbed Alice Mudgarden because Mark Arm of Mudhoney and Chris Cornell of Soundgarden join in on vocals with the boys in AIC. This collaborative effort could even be seen as the predecessor to the *Singles* soundtrack as well considering how many Seattle artists were on that landmark record released in June of 1992.

Still getting used to college life in the summer of 1992, whatever fears and anxieties that were following me around were hushed by what was happening on the global music scene with several of the bands I had been following since my junior and senior years of high school. In addition to that was an unlikely local music scene in the forgotten borough of New York City, Staten Island. As a kid from Brooklyn, the NY scene I knew about was always in Manhattan. Brooklyn was a very long way away from the hipster capital of the world it would become in the 2000s, Queens and the Bronx were hip-hop strongholds, and Staten Island was just the place you drove through to get to New Jersey. There wasn't any real music scene I'd ever heard of coming from the place known mostly for its massive landfill. 1992 would change that perspective.

Music has always been something for me to belong to. When I was a kid, I would get lost in the sounds and rhythms I heard on my mother's radio. As a young teenager, it was the videos, magazine articles, and interviews, along with album covers and posters that would flood my imagination with stories and visuals to go along with the albums and cassettes I would incessantly listen to. Toward the end of high school and the beginning of college, the live experience of being at shows and festivals became my preferred destination on any given night. I belonged to the music and strangely, the artists and the music itself belonged to me.

Along the way, I met like-minded people who experienced music the same way I did, and they became part of the fabric that music wove into the holes in my life where I needed something to fill up the empty spaces. Music, if nothing else, brings people together. The summer of 1992 brought many new people into my life who I still know and am very close with today. This happened in the most unlikely place for a music scene, Staten Island, and with a form of hardcore punk music with a band named Enrage.

Remember the guy in the Misfits t-shirt who spared me from sitting next to the tracksuit guy? Well as it turned out, he was (and still is) the guitarist and main songwriter of Enrage. His name is Mike and alongside him in the band at that time were the singer and drummer brother tandem of Jeff and Marco respectively, and a dude (and future roommate of mine) named Joe on bass. I hadn't heard of Enrage before meeting Mike, but I would come to find out they had quite a following on Staten Island and would eventually go on to play shows with the likes of Bad Brains, Agnostic Front, Type O Negative, Sick of it All, Life of Agony, Biohazard, the Misfits, and dozens more. I was a staple at all their shows throughout the '90s both locally and on the road, (my car was big enough to hold some of the gear so), and being an "insider" in the not-so-underground heavy rock scene in New York made me feel even more connected to what was happening over 3,000 miles away in Seattle. Music creates connections and informs culture. This was happening all around me and the '90s had just barely gotten underway.

The birth of generational music scenes, as well as seismic shifts in culture, do not happen by accident. There are many moving parts making their way throughout society, both seen with the naked eye and simmering somewhere below the surface ready to erupt like a volcano that's been dormant just a bit too long for the earth's liking. A couple of the more common moving parts are a bored and agitated youth population, unstable economic times, abuse of power by governing bodies or institutions, and civil unrest.

In late April and early May of 1992, the United States witnessed the most destructive period of local discord in the history of the country known as the L.A. or Rodney King Riots. Rodney King, a 25-year-old motorist,

CHAPTER 8 - 1992-1993: THIS IS DANGEROUS

was involved in a high-speed chase with the Los Angeles Police Department during the early morning hours of March 3, 1991. The chase began when officers witnessed King's car speed past them and attempted to pull him over. King tried to avoid the officers, and the chase began. After the fact, it would be revealed that King didn't pull over because he had been drinking and was currently on parole. He knew a DUI would violate that parole agreement, so he decided to flee. Upon the eventual stop, King would be beaten by four officers with batons and kicks to the body. The number of baton strikes would equal between 50-60 and King was kicked seven times. All of this is known because of a witness to the entire incident with a video camera. The shocking footage was shown all over the world ad nauseam and the public outcry was one of the loudest I can remember in my lifetime. Making matters worse, King was African American and none of the officers involved were. They were white and Hispanic, and this divided the country down racial lines. Four of the police officers were charged and stood trial for the beating and were subsequently acquitted on April 29, 1992, a little more than a year after the beating took place.

What happened next looked like something straight out of the movies. Upon hearing of the acquittals, people supporting Rodney King took to the streets of L.A. and essentially burned the city down. The riots, lasting through May 4th, would be responsible for the deaths of 63 people, over 2,300 injured, over 12,000 arrests, and more than $1 billion in property damage. And it was all broadcast over the airwaves for the world to see. Fires, brutal attacks on innocent people, destruction of businesses, homes, and cars on every channel for days on end. Welcome to the 1990s where anger, anxiety, isolation, and the need to break free from it all were the hallmarks of the times.

Watching this unfold, I can honestly say I was sickened and saddened by much of what I saw in society and was building an even stronger dislike for humanity than was already inside of me. I was disgusted with racism, abuse of power, and the "old-school" mentality of the Baby Boomer generation, and I needed something that felt like it was my own. Something that had people who thought like I thought to figure out a path forward. Music, and the music scene I was a part of and the one I was watching from afar, was what I turned to.

1992 had some amazing releases that were both sonically incredible and culturally significant. A few that stick out for me were: *Automatic for the People* (R.E.M.), *Dirty* (Sonic Youth), *Sweet Oblivion* (Screaming Trees), *Blind Melon* (Blind Melon), *Check Your Head* (Beastie Boys), *Core* (Stone Temple Pilots), *Piece of Cake* (Mudhoney), *3 Years, 5 Months, and 2 Days in the Life Of. . .* (Arrested Development), *Incesticide* (Nirvana), *Meantime* (Helmet), *Let Me Come Over* (Buffalo Tom), *The Chronic* (Dr. Dre), as well as the records I mentioned earlier in the chapter. The fact that this list of releases followed the list from 1991 is unreal looking back and there was still so much more to come.

Music has always had a way of shaping society and in turn, society has always served as a muse for artists looking for their voices to be heard. One of the biggest shifts in society back in 1992, mainly for young people like me, was the fact that a 46-year-old former Governor of Arkansas (and accomplished saxophone player) named Bill Clinton was about to become the 42nd President of the United States. Politics has more layers to it than I care to discuss. For the context of this book however, it's important that my generation, not knowing much of anything in our late teens, let alone the machinations of the political landscape, had someone entering The White House who seemed to care about them. Where did we get such crazy thoughts? MTV and late-night talk show television of course!

At the time I was less concerned with political parties or his stance on geopolitics but when he was asked "Boxers or Briefs?" on an MTV "Choose or Lose" special designed to prompt young people to vote, how could our generation not love this? If you missed that, maybe you caught the White House hopeful playing Elvis Presley's "Heartbreak Hotel" on the saxophone

CHAPTER 8 - 1992-1993: THIS IS DANGEROUS

during an appearance on the popular Arsenio Hall Show. As we've all grown up and most likely took a deeper and more serious dive into the meat and potatoes of the national and global political landscape, I'd hope stunts like these wouldn't sway us to vote for or against candidates. But for 17- and 18-year-olds in 1992, with our new genre of music pushing us toward relevancy, why wouldn't we vote for someone like Bill Clinton? We did, he got elected, was impeached, and we all moved on.

It's not difficult to connect the dots regarding the timing of how music, culture, the disillusionment of the youth, and a need for change were affecting the lives of young adults everywhere. Here's a quick story about how the new music culture changed life-long habits. I think it's fair to say that holidays are held in high regard for most people. They fall under the category of traditions we typically spend with family. Some folks take certain holidays more seriously than others, but I'd say that New Year's Eve is one of the most celebrated of all the holidays by everyone the world over. The celebrations usually involve family and friends, a big, over-the-top party, and lots of food and drink. None of the New Year's Eve parties I'd ever attended before 1991 were any different from one another. That all changed once I was a part of the new musical revolution.

During the late afternoon on New Year's Eve in either 1991 or 1992, I was in Brooklyn at my home away from home, Ciro's CD Cellar. It was this dingy little store-front record store in Canarsie, a bustling, melting pot of a neighborhood. If it were a bar it would've been Cheers, the fictitious TV sitcom bar where everybody knows your name. There was a decent-sized group of regulars, or "core" customers, of which I was one. I don't know exactly how much money I spent there over the years, but I'm sure it would've amounted to a nice downpayment on a major purchase I could have used years later.

Anyway, it's New Year's Eve Day and the hours just keep passing with music blasting, conversations about the best bands, albums, and shows of the previous weeks, and all was right with the world. As it got close to closing time, probably 6 or 7 PM, and the larger crowd dwindled to maybe five or six of us, including the store owner Ciro, an idea was hatched. I don't remember who suggested it but one of the older guys (probably in his mid-20s) left the store for a few short minutes only to return with a bottle of Jack Daniels, a six-pack of Coca-Cola, and some pretzels and/or chips. Yes, ladies and gentlemen, I, along with a half-dozen other grungy misfits were about to spend New Year's Eve in a tiny, closed record store on Flatlands Avenue in Brooklyn, New York. This couldn't have . . . wouldn't have happened had this new musical revolution not started just a year or two earlier.

I remember telling John Richards, who appeared earlier in the book, this story and he had a great line, "I believe record stores are more important than churches or cathedrals." I agree John, I agree! Nothing before this time could have provoked such emotion or such joy in the feeling of belonging to a movement that was sweeping the world right in front of our eyes. The old way was dead and anything you did now was done as a member of this new club. When you're young, and essentially just living for the moment, you rarely, if ever, pay any attention to the future. Today is all that matters and the level of freedom, and even indestructibility you feel, is the only way you know how to breathe. Spending a holiday in a record store, before 1991, would have sounded completely and utterly insane to just about everyone. After Nirvana took over the world and bands like Pearl Jam, Soundgarden, Alice in Chains, Blind Melon, Jane's Addiction, and so many others became multi-platinum sellers and household names, no one would bat an eye toward my odd New Year's Eve destination, it would barely get a second mention. That's how we lived back then. That's the type of air we were breathing.

"Teenage angst has paid off well, now I'm bored and old," are the first words sung by Kurt Cobain on the first track of perhaps the most anticipated album of all time. *In Utero*, released by DGC Records on September 21, 1993, was Nirvana's third studio album and the follow-up to the generational atom bomb that was *Nevermind*. If anyone was wondering where Cobain's head

CHAPTER 8 - 1992-1993: THIS IS DANGEROUS

was at during the two short years from the time "Smells Like Teen Spirit" became the biggest song in the land until the release of *In Utero*, it wasn't hard to tell. Kurt always seemed to have trouble with his fame yet at the same time looked like he didn't mind, and at times, craved the limelight. He was a complicated figure, to say the least.

Reading into the first line from "Serve The Servants" however, Cobain was certainly not hiding the fact that at the ripe old age of 26, and the life-changing events that followed the release of *Nevermind*, he had soured on the monster that he and his band helped create. What wasn't souring was the attention and sheer manic reaction to Nirvana and grunge music as a whole. If Kurt was over it and ready for something else, the fans of the genre would only grow more fervent by the second.

Vs., the second studio album by another Seattle goliath in the wake of Nirvana's ascension, Pearl Jam, was released by Epic Records a couple of days shy of one month after *In Utero* on October 19, 1993. What happened next would prove that this music, by these bands in this city, no one spoke much of before 1991, would be cemented in the history books forever. In its first week of release, *Vs.* would sell 950,378 copies. Smashing the record previously held by Guns N' Roses and their 1991 album *Use Your Illusion II* which sold 770,000 copies in its first week.

Think about that. Nearly one million records sold in the very first week it was available. To put how big *Vs.* was upon its release into even more perspective, Pearl Jam's second album outperformed all other entries in the Billboard Top Ten that week *combined*! That sales record would stand for five consecutive years until the release of Country music star Garth Brooks's *Double Live* in 1998. This makes sense as by that time, which I will get to in future chapters, grunge had fizzled out.

What I found interesting about both Nirvana's *In Utero* and Pearl Jam's *Vs.* was that both bands intentionally changed the production of these albums drastically when compared to their previous releases. Nirvana and Pearl

Jam were coming from astronomical commercial and critical success with *Nevermind* and *Ten* respectively, in part, due to the slick production both records utilized. *In Utero* and *Vs.* conversely employed edgy, raw, and at times, sloppy production, which gave the records a more visceral feel to them. Both bands would publicly state in interviews many times over that the sound that was achieved on these rawer albums was a truer testament to what the bands were ultimately all about, especially when playing live.

I, for one, can attest to this being true for Pearl Jam as I've seen them live over 30 times since 1992 and what they deliver live is more of the harder, energetic sound we hear on *Vs.* compared to the cleaner-produced sounds from *Ten*. Unfortunately, I never did see Nirvana play live as many of their shows in the early '90s were overseas and sadly I missed the few opportunities I did have to see them in the States. I also agree with Nirvana when they say that *In Utero* (and even their debut album, the very heavy *Bleach*) captured more of who they are as a live band than *Nevermind* did. Regardless of the producers or production stylings, the new genre from Seattle was the dominant force in music and culture by 1993 and it seemed as though it wasn't going to change any time soon.

Not only were important bands releasing big albums in 1993, but Lollapalooza was now a household name and every band, from any genre, that fit the alternative mold at the time, wanted to be a part of its traveling musical parade. As I've mentioned, I attended the first four Lollapalooza tours and my memory of most of those days and performances is still quite good. One band that stood out to me was the "Positive/alternative" Hip-Hop group, Arrested Development. Created in 1988 by rapper/lyricist Speech (Todd Thomas) and DJ Headliner (Timothy Barnwell) in Atlanta, Georgia, Arrested Development, by 1993, would become one of the most popular groups in both Hip-Hop and alternative music. The group's debut album, *3 Years, 5 Months, and 2 Days in the Life Of. . .* was released on March 24, 1992, on Chrysalis/EMI Records and would go on to sell over four million records worldwide and earn

CHAPTER 8 - 1992-1993: THIS IS DANGEROUS

the band two Grammy Awards. I remember falling in love with the record and being blown away when I saw them perform at the 1993 Lollapalooza. I had the good fortune to speak with Speech about those days and how they influenced his career going forward decades later.

When discussing his experience playing Lollapalooza, Speech said, "Playing Lollapalooza back then was just a natural fit for us. I came up listening to more than Hip-Hop. I was listening to Public Enemy and KRS-One of course but I was also listening to Fishbone, Tracy Chapman, Living Colour, and Lenny Kravitz, so there was a lot of that viewpoint and discipline that I was already influenced by. Lollapalooza was the first time we had a chance to play in front of a predominantly white audience and it helped us (and the audience) understand and find love in one another."

Music has so many layers and bands and listeners alike pick through and find the layers they identify with the most which helps them determine what they love about certain bands or artists. For me, though, it always does find its way back to the songs. I hear some songs and then I *feel* some songs. The songs I *feel* are the ones I know contain the good stuff. The stuff you can't quite put into words and yet your soul just seems to know that that song belongs in a special place.

Arrested Development has a song like that for me and it's their smash hit, "Tennessee," off their debut album and prominently played throughout the early and mid-'90s all over MTV, radio, and stages across the globe. The track, with its infectious, shoulder-sway-inducing drum loop, gut-wrenching rhythm, and blunt and heartfelt lyrics, is a history lesson, a plea for help, an escape route, and an exercise in blind faith and hope all wrapped up into one. It's fucking brilliant.

"I've always written in that direct style," said Speech, and he continued, "Because I see so many problems in this world that are a result of a lack of communication and a lack of people just talking to each other and saying the things that need to be said. *Tennessee* was a gift. It was a gift from my grandmother who passed away and she was from Tennessee. As well as my brother who passed a week after she did. The last place I saw both of them was in Tennessee. I believe that when people you love pass, they pass onto you certain attributes, certain things that you start to develop or gain interest in. It's a weird phenomenon but I've seen it more times than I can tell you. I think they passed on something that made that song come out of me so easily. I was deeply hurt and yes, that song has made me cry, but it's still a celebratory song and we have a great time performing it even though it does come from the loss of two incredible people. I know a lot of people who have been through deep loss also feel that song in a special way."

Speech looks back on the early days of his career in Arrested Development and knows that special moment in time, the late '80s/early '90s, planted the seeds for a lifetime. Arrested Development continues to release albums and tour the world, and Speech has also become a documentary filmmaker, including his film, "16 Bars," about making music with inmates in a Virginia jail.

Musically, things seemed to be heading in a positive direction, but the U.S. was dealing with some violent events in 1993 as it was witness to both the first World Trade Center bombing in New York City and the standoff between the Bureau of Alcohol, Tobacco, and Firearms and the leader and followers of a religious cult in Waco, Texas called the Branch Davidians. In both incidents combined 15 people were killed (six in the World Trade Center bombing and nine in the raid in Waco) and over 1,000 were injured. We weren't quite in the digital age yet but the nightly news media, both local and national outlets, were chomping at the bit to see who could show the most shocking and gory images to gain market share.

Along with the L.A. Riots a year earlier, violence on TV and throughout the media had become the norm, and people, especially young Gen Xers, were getting sick of it all. The anger and frustration were certainly evident in the music and the decade was barely underway. This is one of the areas where

CHAPTER 8 - 1992-1993: THIS IS DANGEROUS

it's hard to reconcile the abundance of great music, creating a brand-new culture that a generation could call its own with the place it came from. Anger, despair, violence, drug addiction, and boredom. It was combustible, to say the least and in hindsight, was never meant to last.

CHAPTER 9 – 1994
THE SHOT HEARD AROUND THE WORLD: CRASH OF THE KING AND THE PENDING DOOM

"I DON'T FUCKING BELIEVE THIS; KURT COBAIN IS DEAD. HE SHOT HIMSELF," I SAID TO MY friend Mike on the phone. "He's dead," I repeated. "I know," Mike replied. "I just saw it on TV. Wow."

The news of Kurt's suicide spread like wildfire on April 8, 1994, but the announcement I remember most was by MTV's Kurt Loder with a somber, almost stunned, broadcast of the tragic event. My reaction, along with Mike's, Loder's, and millions more as we'd all soon see, was the epitome of collective, cultural grief. We were angry, disaffected kids with cynicism and disdain for anything other than our scene but this news, this death, triggered something beyond all of that. Sadness, confusion, and an odd "what the fuck do we do now" moment.

I realize some people don't understand and even ridicule those of us who are seriously affected by the loss of people we don't know personally, and that's ok. I'm not trying to change anyone into thinking or feeling like I do. I understand why some folks are ambivalent about the death of strangers. For me though, music isn't a stranger at all, and the people who create the music that hits me the hardest, feel like family. Not in the traditional way of course, but the family of the chosen variety. I can guarantee that I "know" some of my favorite musicians more than certain blood relatives. I know this because artists give you clues as to who they are. They do so through their music, lyrics, books, poems, paintings, and so forth. A connection is made. Some blood relatives, on the other hand, the furthest I've ever got with them is the simple fact that I know their names and where they live, sometimes. That's it. So, tell me again why I shouldn't experience a level of grief when someone I'm connected with dies, especially so violently and at their own hand.

For his fans, and fans of the entire grunge and alternative music scene in the '90s, Kurt's suicide opened deep wounds within all of us. If Kurt could kill himself, who amongst us couldn't?

An interesting phenomenon happens when someone who is culturally significant, famous, and put up on a pedestal by much of society dies. Many people feel like they've lost a loved one and I've always found this to be fascinating. My earliest recollection of this stems from the December 8, 1980, assassination of John Lennon. I was only 7 ½ years old when it happened but the man was a Beatle, and the news coverage was constant. I remember the candlelight vigils and videos of people gathering in public places singing Beatles songs. It stuck with me. It made an impact.

April 8, 1994, was the date that many people from my generation had their own experience of grieving the loss of someone they never knew but somehow felt like they did. It was the date the world learned that Kurt Cobain, the 27-year-old leader of the biggest band in the world and reluctant spokesman of a very fucked up generation, was dead. Cobain had taken his own life with a shotgun blast to the head on April 5th in a room above the garage of his Seattle home. About a month earlier on March 4th, Kurt was hospitalized in Rome, Italy after overdosing on Benzodiazepines and alcohol. Nirvana's management company put out a statement saying the overdose was accidental but others close to the singer, namely his wife Courtney Love and

CHAPTER 9 - 1994: THE SHOT HEARD AROUND THE WORLD

his cousin who was a nurse, both believe the overdose was an attempted suicide.

In a piece written by David Fricke for *Rolling Stone* magazine, Courtney Love said of the OD, "He took 50 pills. He probably forgot how many he took. But there was a definite suicidal urge." In a story that appeared on Consumer Health Day, Cobain's cousin Beverly (the nurse) mentioned that the family had a history of suicide, and that Kurt had previously been diagnosed with attention deficit hyperactivity disorder as well as bipolar disorder. Many of Kurt's lyrics had bipolar disorderedly foreshadowing and acknowledgments of depression in them as well.

Tracks such as "Lithium," "All Apologies," "Negative Creep," "Dumb," and the prophetically titled, "I Hate Myself and Want to Die" would all count as examples of that mindset. That last song was Kurt's original title for the album *In Utero* but was thankfully talked out of it by bassist and Nirvana co-founder, Krist Novocelic. The song never did make it onto any of Nirvana's studio albums but was included on the *Beavis and Butt-Head Experience* compilation album as well as Nirvana's rarities boxset, *With the Lights Out*. The track was also scheduled to be the B-side on the band's "Pennyroyal Tea" single, but that release was shelved after Cobain's death. Kurt's messaging in certain songs was what struck such a lasting chord with so many kids.

"It allowed kids going through the same things," says Joseph J. Williams, LMHC, A-CBT, "to share a universality of suffering, a universality of understanding. These kids no longer felt alone."

I was approaching my 21st birthday when the news of the Nirvana frontman's death exploded through my television and radio speakers on that early April day. I remember feeling equal parts sad, angry, confused, and defeated. I'm not a psychologist so I cannot explain why I felt these emotions, I just knew I did.

Going back to Joseph J. Williams, for some clinical perspective on this very topic, he said, "I had conversations about the death of artists such as

Kurt and more recently Chester Bennington (Linkin Park), with clients who were fans of theirs. From those conversations, I can say that although the relationship was not physical, it still hurts to lose someone who (as my clients put it) 'understood me, who understood my struggle, who wasn't afraid to come forward. Someone who believed in the same thing as me, cause, ideal, values.'" Kurt and his music attracted those who might have been socially isolated, increasing the importance of his role in their lives, and making the loss more prominent. Artists like Kurt are in a way a source of support and understanding for people and to lose that can be very painful even if they never come face to face with the person. The benefit of artists recording their work is that they can continue to support people even after they are gone. Like relatives looking at their lost loved ones in pictures or reading cards they might have sent them with inspiring words while they were still with us, fans can look back and continue to hear the artists' message in their music."

I wasn't alone in my state of mind as countless millions the world over were feeling the same things. At 50 years old I can now look back at my almost 21-year-old self in 1994 and see that kid was lost. I'd argue that most 20-year-olds share similar feelings of confusion, despair, fear, and in some cases, sadness about their lives at that time. So much is ahead of us at that age and yet we've learned very few real-life skills by that point. I'd also argue that most kids between the ages of 18-22 haven't experienced all that much loss of life and probably view death as something that happens to other people in other families.

Music is tremendously important to young people all over the planet and when a new genre and scene comes along that unquestionably defines a generation . . . *your* generation, you hold onto those who created it all in such high regard, they somehow become like a member of your own family. I even believe that Kurt Cobain himself held certain artists in that high regard as well. He often professed his love for The Beatles and other bands he was influenced by. There's even a lyric in "Serve the Servants" off *In Utero* that I've

CHAPTER 9 – 1994: THE SHOT HEARD AROUND THE WORLD

always believed to be a shout-out to Perry Farrell of Jane's Addiction and their song "Had a Dad" off their 1988 album *Nothing's Shocking*, proving his lofty admiration for him and his band. The lyric goes, "I tried hard to have a father but instead I had a dad."

Kurt's parents divorced when he was a young boy, and he did not have much of a relationship with his father after that. In my eyes, this line was Kurt's way of saying that he missed and needed his father who wasn't there, but music was, and that's what he turned to as a replacement.

So, when someone of Kurt's stature and importance dies, especially by his own hands, you can be damn sure that the generation of lost souls who looked up to that person will struggle with the flood of emotions they're suddenly faced with. There's so much more that can be said about the time leading up to and after Cobain's death. For this book though, the fact that he died (and how he died) at the height of his fame, not to mention the height of the scene he helped create, is what began the downfall, at least commercially, of the grunge movement. The downfall wasn't so much in that people no longer wanted to hear this music or somehow changed their mindsets regarding how they viewed the world and the things they were personally going through, not at all. If anything, they needed this music now more than ever.

Kurt's death, in and of itself, did not end the grunge and alternative music movement. The record companies who feared that Kurt's death would also kill the cash cow that Kurt was partially responsible for were the ones who killed the scene. They did this by ratcheting up their efforts to sign the "next" Nirvana and replace Kurt with someone else, tenfold. They initially tried to make Pearl Jam frontman, Eddie Vedder, the new poster child and all that did was nearly break up that group. So, when that plan failed, they signed anyone and everyone who could scream, yell, wear flannel, Doc Martens, and maybe learn a few guitar chords.

The oversaturation was felt far and wide and so many of the bands and songs that were coming out after this record label feeding frenzy started to become more of a parody rather than a continuation of what the scene was all about. That didn't mean though that amazing and important music had stopped being released, quite the opposite.

1994 will always be remembered as the year Kurt Cobain died and as some have lazily put it, the year that grunge died. With the releases I'm about to list below, I'd like to think they can stand as proof that not only was the scene not dying, but it was only getting better. Kurt may have died but the scene that was largely built on his band's success was alive and well. A man died but a legend was born. You must remember; we're talking about a time in the music industry when album sales meant everything. This was the pre-digital age, pre-social media, and pre-streaming. Those changes were coming and coming quickly but in 1994, no one knew that. So, it was still incredibly important for artists to write and release albums at a quick pace, market and sell those albums with music videos, touring, merchandise, and media interaction such as TV, print, and radio interviews.

It wasn't like today when an artist can post a message or release a song on YouTube, Instagram, X (formerly Twitter), Facebook, or via their website all while interacting with their entire fan base literally whenever they want. It was a much different world in the '90s and for an artist or band to remain relevant and continue to have the resources to release albums and tour the world, they needed to play the music industry games. With that in mind, it's no wonder so many great albums came out in 1994 by artists who are still important today.

In my opinion (and in no particular order) these are some of the most important releases of 1994:

Superunknown (Soundgarden), *MTV Unplugged in New York* (Nirvana), *The Downward Spiral* (Nine Inch Nails), *Ill Communication* (Beastie Boys), *Jar of Flies* (Alice In Chains), *Vitalogy* (Pearl Jam), *Under The Pink* (Tori Amos), *Rubberneck* (Toadies), *Definitely Maybe* (Oasis), *Monster* (R.E.M.), *Live Through This* (Hole), *Ready to Die* (The Notorious B.I.G.), *Grace* (Jeff

CHAPTER 9 - 1994: THE SHOT HEARD AROUND THE WORLD

Buckley), *Purple* (Stone Temple Pilots), *Stranger Than Fiction* (Bad Religion), *Throwing Copper* (Live), *Weezer* (AKA The Blue Album, Weezer), *Mellow Gold* (Beck), *Korn* (Korn), *American Thighs* (Veruca Salt), *Illmatic* (Nas), *Sixteen Stone* (Bush), *Whiskey for the Holy Ghost* (Mark Lanegan), *Dookie* (Green Day).

For so many reasons, the records listed above made big impressions on me but also the music community at large. Some were amazing debuts that would establish successful new genres (Korn, Biggie, and Nas), others were continuations of the grunge movement (Soundgarden, Pearl Jam, Nirvana, AIC), Hole, Tori Amos, and Veruca Salt would start to put women in rock in the forefront and set the stage for what would happen over the next few years as female artists skyrocketed to prominence.

The biggest commercial and cultural record for the alternative music community released that year was *Dookie* by Green Day. Released by Reprise Records on February 1, 1994, *Dookie* was Green Day's third studio album, but its major label debut. This was a very significant distinction back in the '90s and certainly for a genre such as punk rock. Green Day formed in San Francisco, California in 1987 and released two albums (*39/Smooth* and *Kerplunk*) before *Dookie* with Lookout Records, a local independent record label. Going back to the early days of punk and all independent/underground music, there were some unwritten rules that bands had to abide by to stay in the good graces of the fan bases that followed from their very beginnings. The worst thing an underground band, especially in punk music, could do, is sign with a major record label. They were deemed "sellouts" if they did and virtually abandoned by most of their earliest and most passionate fans.

When Green Day released Dookie with Reprise and especially when it became the absolute monster hit it did, the band was forever ostracized from its original fan base and had to defend itself in interviews for years afterward. Green Day wasn't bothered by this in the least as they laughed their way straight to the bank.

So many of the bands listed above have either become household names in music and/or have influenced an untold number of bands who came after. One band that I feel deserves more credit than they tend to receive is the Toadies. In 1989, singer/guitarist Vaden Todd Lewis, bassist Lisa Umbarger, guitarist Darrel Herbert, and drummer Mark Reznicek, formed the Toadies in Fort Worth, Texas. Partially influenced by what was happening in Seattle based on pure timing, the Toadies' larger influences came from bands like Led Zeppelin, ZZ Top, Talking Heads, and the Pixies. It was this varied group of influences and not just the sounds coming from Seattle that gave the band its distinctly unique sound.

In 2022, alongside a great writer and podcast host, Keith R. Higgons, I had the pleasure of co-hosting the Abandoned Albums podcast for about a year with Keith. We were lucky enough to have Vaden from the Toadies on with us in March of '22 and he talked about what it was like to be in a band in the mid-'90s that not only was a constant on MTV and alternative and rock radio but had recorded one of the most popular and enduring albums of the decade, *Rubberneck*. Hits such as "Tyler," "I Come from the Water," "Backslider," and the omnipresent "Possum Kingdom" were staples during the mid and late '90s and the band sold millions of records and toured the world due to the success of its debut album.

"I went into that first record thinking I'd get to make the ideal Toadies record that I wanted to make in a real studio, with real producers, go on tour, get to see the states, play some rock 'n' roll , meet some cool people, then get dropped from the label, go home, and go back to working at the record store," said Lewis. If Lewis did go back to the record store he worked at before forming the Toadies, it would be as a customer and not an employee.

What made the band interesting to me was the unique sound they had (in my mind it was Black Sabbath, meets, ZZ Top, meets the Pixies) mixed with the dark storytelling of Vaden's lyrics. During our Abandoned Albums podcast, Keith and I discussed this with Lewis, and he told us that he became

CHAPTER 9 – 1994: THE SHOT HEARD AROUND THE WORLD

a fan of the creative writing, horror genre made famous by Stephen King and the twisted poetry of Edgar Allan Poe.

Songs like "Tyler" and "Possum Kingdom" off *Rubberneck* and "Jigsaw Girl" off the band's sophomore effort, *Hell Below/Stars Above*, were morbid love songs that ended in murder in the fashion of a possible serial killer. With all the songs about depression, drug addiction, isolation, and suicide coming from the Seattle scene, tracks like these about lovelorn serial killers were a breath of fresh air. Those words, in that order, were likely never written before and perhaps I'm a little darker than I know I already am. Moving on.

I was a fan from the first time I heard the Toadies and now that I had the opportunity to speak with Vaden, I asked him about his musical influences since his band's sound was quite different from what was happening back in the early '90s. "I worked in a record store in Texas when I was young but before I was employed there, I was a customer. I grew up listening to the same rock music we all did, and I was ready for something different. I walked into the store one day and asked them to show me the weirdest thing they could. The first thing they played me was the Talking Heads and they put *77* in my hand and that blew my mind. It was the weirdest thing I'd ever heard. I went from there to The Cure and then the Pixies came out. That just changed everything."

The Pixies were always *that* band that turned rock music fans into something else. They had a different sensibility of timing and melody, and they utilized the soft/loud/soft song dynamics better than anyone had at the time. Kurt Cobain always cited them as one of his biggest influences as a songwriter. You can hear it in Nirvana's songs, you can hear it in Toadies songs, and almost everyone else who played a version of hard and alternative rock in the 1990s. The Toadies went on to sell over a million copies of Rubberneck and have released seven studio albums to date. Vaden and the band are still writing, recording, and touring and they are a must-see live band.

Turning 21 has always been seen as a milestone birthday in the United States. This is the year people are legally classified as adults. When you're 18 or 19 and the big 2 1 is in sight, you almost wish time travel existed so you could skip the couple of years that are on your way to becoming an adult so you can finally do whatever you'd like. It sounds silly now but back then, the quicker "adulthood" arrived, the better off you'd be. Not so fast skippy, be careful what you wish for. Heaping the responsibility of adulthood on someone who is either still in college or living in their parents' house is a flawed and ill-conceived concept in my opinion. I can only speak for myself and those around me at the time, but there was no possible way that I would (or did) consider myself an adult in 1994. The mere thought of it was and is ludicrous.

With college graduation still a year away (two in my case as I blew out the ACL in my left knee in 1995 and couldn't graduate on time due to the surgery, no Zoom classes in those days), and realizing my internship at Epic Records probably wasn't going to lead to a full-time job with the label, I was utterly lost. All I wanted to do was to have a career in the music industry in some way, shape, or form, but with each passing month, that prospect seemed bleak.

The world has always had a way of distracting us from our individual lives, and on June 17, 1994, I along with about 95 million other people, were distracted from our lives in a way we had never seen before. Orenthal James (O.J.) Simpson, American Pro Football Hall of Fame running back turned actor and celebrity, magically appeared on televisions across the country, interrupting Game 5 of the NBA Finals between the Houston Rockets and the New York Knicks. Being the huge Knicks fan that I am, I was watching the game intently (the Knicks won the game but ultimately lost the series), living and dying with each possession, and suddenly my television was no longer showing an NBA Finals game and instead forced me to watch a white, Ford Bronco, embroiled in a low-speed police chase on a California freeway.

CHAPTER 9 - 1994: THE SHOT HEARD AROUND THE WORLD

Most people alive today have heard of or seen footage of this event, as it was happening in real-time, however, it was absolutely one of the strangest and most confusing things anyone had witnessed, live on television. Simpson was the main suspect in the double murder of his ex-wife Nicole Brown Simpson and her friend Ron Goldman. The friends were found stabbed to death outside of Nicole's condo in Brentwood, a neighborhood in Los Angeles, California on June 12, 1994. O.J. Simpson would eventually be charged with both murders and ultimately acquitted of all charges on October 3, 1995, which was dubbed "the trial of the century."

While many people believe O.J. did kill both Ron and Nicole, the bizarre trial was fraught with racial overtones, odd behavior by most involved, constant media coverage, and countless conspiracy theories. No additional arrests or convictions regarding the murders have been made to this day.

Now in the mid-'90s, we Gen Xers had more than our share of violence on TV. War, riots, murders, and trials were commonplace, and desensitization was setting in. It was around this time that I noticed a feeling that I first felt when I was about nine years old. It came in waves, but this time it was different. It was deep and palpable. I had become depressed and was beginning to have trouble seeing the purpose in my life.

CHAPTER 10 – 1995-1996
CAPITALIZING ON IT ALL: THE ADVERTISING WORLD WAS NOT READY FOR IT TO BE OVER

"I WISH I KNEW SOMEONE IN CALIFORNIA," SAID A VERY ATTRACTIVE FEMALE COLLEGE CLASSmate of mine as we walked across campus on a crisp New York October morning. "Why is that?" I replied. "Well, today is the day we're gonna find out what the verdict will be in the O.J. case."

For those who don't know, O.J. Simpson, NFL Hall of Famer, turned famous actor, turned . . . criminal, was on trial for the murders of his ex-wife, Nicole Brown Simpson, and Ron Goldman, a waiter and friend of Nicole's. "Oh, right," I said to my friend, not too sure where this conversation was headed. "So, because of the time difference between NY & L.A., they're going to know the verdict before we do."

I know what you're thinking, and you're right. I should've explained how time zones actually work, and that California did not, in fact, exist in a time machine, but I was a shallow, testosterone-filled college student and this girl was gorgeous. So, with the hopes of not embarrassing her, all I could muster up as a response was, "Yeah . . . I wish I knew someone in California too." What can I say? I'm just a mere mortal, right?

That light-hearted conversation aside, the mid-'90s were shaping up to be pretty dark for Me. I tore the ACL in my left knee in 1995 which required surgery and caused me to graduate from college a semester late. I was already scared to hit the "real world" as I knew deep down that I didn't have any real career skills to speak of and was not interested in taking any of the civil servant's tests that so many kids were taking. Both of my parents were city workers, and they seemed miserable. Plus, they're the ones who wanted me to get a college degree in the first place, so I didn't have to get a city job. None of it made sense to me and I was not excited about my future whatsoever.

On top of my personal issues, 1995 also gave witness to yet another act of terrorism in our country. This time it was of the domestic variety when Timothy McVeigh and Terry Nichols, two U.S. Army veterans, blew up the Alfred E. Murrah Federal Building in Oklahoma City, Oklahoma. My reality at this time felt like the title of the 1994 album by Nine Inch Nails, *The Downward Spiral*.

When people talk about the '90s, the early to mid-'90s specifically, they tend to talk about grunge. A dark, introspective, and in some cases, drug-induced genre from the Pacific Northwest which was overwhelmingly male. Time will typically leave some things out and create narratives that aren't all that accurate. Did the grunge movement take over and rule the world from a musical point of view for a time? It did. It's the basis for this book and for discussions surrounding that time musically and culturally. Just as with anything in life though, things get left out.

One of the best things that came out of the '90s music explosion was the plethora of female singers, all-female bands, or female-fronted bands it spawned. It was sorely needed and ultimately very influential. A global superstar in 2023 like Olivia Rodrigo covered the 1994 mega-hit "Seether" by Veruca Salt on her first major tour and instantaneously introduced millions of kids to a song (and band) their parents have been listening to for 28 years.

Every decade has its carryover from previous decades because there's always an icon or two who's not quite ready to go quietly into oblivion. Ma-

CHAPTER 10 - 1995-1996: CAPITALIZING ON IT ALL

donna is the perfect example of a superstar from the '80s who was just hitting her stride in the '90s but she wasn't a product of that decade. The '90s did however foster some incredibly creative, talented, and several highly successful female artists in all genres. Quickly coming to mind is Mariah Carey, Britney Spears, Mary J. Blige, etc. These women were all over the pop and R&B charts throughout the decade and sold millions upon millions of records. There was an entirely different version of influential and successful female artists though and they broke through in genres that weren't necessarily synonymous with commercial success or enabled women to thrive. I'm referring to the boy's club that is typically punk, hardcore, alternative, hip-hop, metal, and grunge. Due to the success of Nirvana's *Nevermind*, the floodgates opened for everyone, and women provided some of the best and most powerful music of the decade.

The terms "grunge" and "alternative" are very broad and oftentimes confusing descriptions of what a band or artist may sound like. I understand why labels are given to sounds and why genres are discussed with titles because it's just easier for the sake of conversation. It wouldn't be practical to discuss music and then describe the tone, feel, or sound of the music to let the people know what you are talking about. It's easier to simply say, "pop," "dance," "rock" or "jazz." Inherently though, these labels become misleading, subjective, and sometimes flat-out inaccurate when describing music. This is how I view most of the labels that female musicians were given during the '90s, especially when just lazily lumped into "alternative."

Artists such as Tori Amos, Liz Phair, and Fiona Apple were all '90s staples yet quite different from one another. They all fell into that "alternative" bucket, but each had a unique sound and musical style which usually did not sound anything like their counterparts. The same thing happened with men too, specifically with grunge. The four most popular male bands with the grunge moniker were Nirvana, Pearl Jam, Soundgarden, and Alice in Chains, yet none of them sounded anything like the other. Again though, I understand why these names were used but it does lead to some confusion and even more than a few omissions from the scene 30-plus years later.

Names and titles aside, the female artists who began or broke through in the '90s laid a foundation for future generations of girls to understand that it was perfectly fine for females to pick up guitars, drumsticks, or microphones and thrash the hell out of them just like the guys did. You didn't even have to be a solo artist or an all-girl band to influence and succeed. Bands like Hole, No Doubt, Bikini Kill, Garbage, L7, Babes in Toyland, The Cranberries, The Breeders, and so many others rocked stages and released records all over the world to millions of fans.

Life-long careers were created for many of these women, both on stage or behind the scenes as songwriters or producers for other musicians. The rise of female artists in the '90s got so big there was a festival created specifically for women called Lilith Fair. Like Lollapalooza before it, Lilith Fair was a touring festival created by a successful and influential artist looking to showcase the talents of bands and artists who inspired her.

Sarah McLachlan, a Canadian singer/songwriter, who was and is, one of the most commercially successful female artists of her generation, along with Dan Fraser and Terry McBride, created the festival in 1997. Due to the success of tours such as Lollapalooza and The Warped Tour, Lilith Fair knew it had an audience ready and waiting for them. Female musicians have not been given their proper due for so long, let alone getting to create and run a festival of their own, the Lilith Fair exemplifies how important the '90s were for female artists.

It wasn't just rock or alternative music that benefited from this rise in female artistry. Hip-hop, which was breaking big throughout the mid and late '80s, saw a massive rise in popularity in the '90s. This was in no small part due to artists like Queen Latifah, Lauryn Hill, Lil' Kim, Missy Elliott, and '80s holdovers Salt-N-Pepa, who had some of the biggest songs and albums of the entire decade.

CHAPTER 10 - 1995-1996: CAPITALIZING ON IT ALL

In a book like this, that discusses a decade as prolific as the '90s were, some names are bound to be left out. I'm writing this, not just from a commercial and cultural significance point of view, but also a bit of a subjective one. Our musical tastes are all subjective so it's naive to think we will all agree on everything in this book or others like it. The best I can do is talk about what happened during the '90s, some of the more important or well-known figures who helped create what happened and add my two cents about the entire scene. The juxtaposition between some of the biggest names in music against lesser-known ones wasn't as much of a big deal in the '90s as it may have been in previous decades or music scenes. I'm not saying that everyone was on equal footing, that wouldn't be true. What I am saying though is that the culture that existed throughout the '90s, particularly in the early and middle portions of the decade, allowed for famous people and those not as famous to coexist and carve out careers within the music industry.

In 1995, a newly widowed Courtney Love and her band Hole performed as one of the headlining acts on that year's Lollapalooza tour. By all accounts, and probably understandably so considering the still very open wound of her husband Kurt Cobain's recent suicide, Love was under a ton of pressure which resulted in odd behavior throughout the tour.

Quoted in an article for *Stereogum*, Hole guitarist Eric Erlandson had this to say about the start of the tour, "We had bulk candy backstage, and I go, 'there's Kathleen Hanna (frontwoman for Bikini Kill), you should offer her some candy.' She grabbed the candy and just threw it at her. Everybody was like, 'Oh my God, she just punched her in the face.' But from what I saw she just threw the candy and kind of slapped her in the direction of her face. I don't know if she actually hit her or what, it doesn't matter, it was not cool. The whole tour started on that note."

Hole's bassist, Melissa Auf der Maur, said in the same article, "I was saddened by what I almost perceived as Sonic Youth's (the tour's official headliner) bullying of Courtney. That lady was a widow, and she was on a survival path after a very traumatic moment in her life, and I didn't think the cool kids should be bullying and picking on her. She was an easy target . . . I never would have thought that Lee (Lee Renaldo, member of Sonic Youth) would speak against her because Lee was always very nice. I just remember hearing, like, Sonic Youth is blogging and dissing Courtney."

Also on this tour was a young, female singer for a little-known but ferocious hardcore punk band called Thorazine, named Jo-Ann Rogan. I caught up with Jo-Ann, a native New Yorker (but coming of age in Philadelphia, Pennsylvania) to discuss this very Lollapalooza tour, how she became interested in this wave of '90s music, and her subsequent career in Thorazine.

"I can remember people getting into the Melvins," said Rogan, "in the late '80s in West Philly and that's where I first remembered hearing 'grunge.' The music was so slow and heavy, grungy. Soon after that, it all just went nuts. I'd always wanted to sing for a punk band, but this was the late '80s and my friends would all say that I needed to learn how to play bass because no one's going to let you front a punk band. I said, 'fuck that.'"

Jo-Ann was just like the other musicians I'd read about and spoken with, whose carefree and take no shit attitude is what helped propel them to become a part of the music they loved. For so many, the mid- and late-'80s underground movement truly was the spark that lit the fuse.

"Nobody wanted to play with me," Rogan continued, "except these outcast dudes (her eventual bandmates in Thorazine) and that's how I got into Thorazine in the first place. We wound up touring for years, and years, and years."

Although the '90s were more inclusive than other eras, it was still relatively uncommon for a female to lead such a heavy band as Thorazine. "I was a woman in a hardcore band," Rogan said. "I was touring with the likes of Fear, ANTiSEEN, and The Murder Junkies, not everyone accepted me. It all depended on where we were and when. Tampa, Florida hated us, Southern

CHAPTER 10 - 1995-1996: CAPITALIZING ON IT ALL

Texas loved us. We did great in L.A. Also, our drummer was black so were a bi-racial, female-fronted band. It was a crapshoot."

Jo-Ann and I went on to discuss their time on the Lollapalooza tour and the story is something out of a movie. Before embarking on the tour in 1995, She said, "At the time of Lollapalooza, we were getting sued by Smith-Kline Beechum (one of the largest pharmaceutical companies in the world at the time) over the band's name." Thorazine, an antipsychotic medication that treats mental health conditions, nausea, vomiting, and anxiety, was a product put out by Smith-Kline Beechum.

Rogan continued, "We're this little band from Philly with a 7-inch out (a vinyl single) and we get this cease-and-desist letter from this mammoth company. Next thing you know, the *Philadelphia Enquirer* did a huge story that went out on the *AP Newswire*. Now I've got lawyers calling me from New York, it was just everywhere. I was bartending at night and then waking up very early in the morning to do national radio shows about the lawsuit, it was nuts. That's when Lollapalooza called, and we headlined one of the side stages. This was my first band, and it was all crazy magical. Reality struck though because we were playing the same show where Courtney Love had shotgun shells thrown at her on stage. This was real life."

I think one of the biggest, if not the biggest examples of female influence (commercially and in changing the narrative for what a woman can accomplish in a male-dominated musical scene) was that of Gwen Stefani of the band No Doubt. It's hard to argue with the band's commercial success as they've sold between 30-40 million records worldwide, most of those sales coming in the '90s. The first and most relevant incarnation of the band was from 1986-2004 with the bulk of their influence and popularity coming during the 1990s.

Musically the band was a mix of ska, punk, and pop music, with more hooks and melodies than you might imagine. It's hard to predict when certain sounds and bands will cut through the noise and seemingly overnight, take over. We know their success didn't occur overnight, same as Nirvana's didn't, but to the world at large, these bands came out of nowhere and still hold relevance today. That is not only extremely difficult to do but also highly uncommon for music that isn't straight-up pop.

During the height of the MTV era (late '80s - mid-'90s), no one should underestimate the influence that videos had over the entire music industry. We're told as a society that looks do not matter and we shouldn't judge a book by its cover, but we know that's not very practical. It may be the right thing to do but it's not necessarily a part of human nature. Unfortunately, when it comes to female artists the scales are always tipped in favor of looks more so than talent. It's a bit of a double-edged sword because sometimes looks will get you in the door and talent will keep you in the room. In the case of Gwen Stefani, she had the looks that guys loved, the fashion and image that girls wanted to emulate, and the talent to break through it all.

Gwen's sense of melody, along with the band's implementation of ska and punk blended with pop sensibilities proved to be a recipe for success. Watching them perform these songs on television all around the globe through their videos propelled the band from Anaheim, California into the stratosphere of rock stardom. Their success was vital to the scene as they were a major reason why other female-fronted bands started springing up everywhere. It was also why young girls watching at home decided that becoming a rock star was now possible for them.

Listening to Gwen sing "Just a Girl" off 1995's *Tragic Kingdom*, with its satirical lyrics about how girls can't do anything by themselves, lit a fuse that led to millions of young girls bouncing in unison to the song's beat and message. The song still resonates to this day and will likely serve as a female anthem for as long as music is around.

Every generation has its cultural significance. Music has always been closely tied to the events and lifestyles of the people living in those genera-

CHAPTER 10 - 1995-1996: CAPITALIZING ON IT ALL

tions. Depending on someone's age, geographical location, and stage of life they're in at the time, the music of that generation has varying effects on those who hear it. Not only did the '90s have a cultural impact on all who lived through the decade, but it can be argued that due to the huge shift in music from the late '80s to the start of the '90s, this decade had the biggest cultural impact since the 1960s.

Another massive record that sent a female artist into the stratosphere of superstardom was *Jagged Little Pill* by Alanis Morisette. Released on June 13, 1995, on Madonna's label Maverick, the third studio album by Canadian-born Morisette became a focal point of the music industry and female fans around the globe. Not unlike *Tragic Kingdom*, *Jagged Little Pill* served as a wake-up call that women had just as much to say and could rock as hard as their male counterparts. In Morissette's case, this was most evident in the album's lead single, "You Oughta Know." A scathing retort to a lover who betrayed Alanis, "You Oughta Know"' *was*, and still is, a worldwide proclamation for women everywhere who have been through a messy breakup but won't go quietly into the night.

The sheer grit and visceral emotion that pours from the song is as strong as anything that came from the '90s. If you listen to music now, in the 2020s, it seems normal to hear very blunt and direct lyrics from female artists singing about all sorts of topics. In 1995 however, this type of in-your-face content, especially regarding anything relating to sex or power coming from a woman was rare. Almost nonexistent in commercial music.

The reaction when this song first came out was as if no one had ever heard a woman say the things that Alanis Morissette said in her lyrics. Some people were appalled but so many more were liberated. This was an awakening. "You Oughta Know" *was* permission for anyone to say anything. Especially if you were a female musician who was trying her hardest to not censor her true feelings. It was both a revelation and a revolution at the same time.

Most of the uproar came from a few provocative lines from the song with phrases like "go down on you" and "thinking of me when you fuck her" and you get the idea.

These lyrics were hard-hitting, in your face, and unequivocally unapologetic. It's exactly what was needed to send this new and fearless music into the public consciousness. It was impossible to ignore the impact a song like "You Oughta Know" had upon its release. It set the tone for every female musician who had something to say and wanted to do so without any restrictions.

In sticking with the theme of female artists who did and said whatever was on their minds, I had the pleasure of speaking with Tracy Bonham, whose single, "Mother Mother" off her debut album, *The Burdens of Being Upright* dominated MTV and the Billboard charts in 1996. The gritty, yet melodic track was written from the perspective of a young woman facing the world for the first time, independent of parental control. It comes across as a letter or a conversation between a daughter who needs to find her way and a mom who doesn't want to let go or even know the truth about her child's new life.

The dynamics in both the sonic performance of the song musically and how Tracy's voice delivers the sharp and witty lyrics, highlighted by her infamous primal scream in the chorus, is nothing short of anthemic angst and a perfect sign of the times. I'll go so far as to say that Tracy's scream of the lyric "Everything's fine" in the chorus is one of the best and most effective screams to define the feelings of the entire generation.

I originally spoke with the twice-nominated Grammy Award artist, as the co-host of the Abandoned Albums Podcast with Keith R. Higgons. Because Tracy was so engaging and informative on that show, I wanted to speak with her specifically about the book as well. Although Bonham was born in Eugene, Oregon, the singer-songwriter and multi-instrumentalist would cite the thriving underground scene in Boston, Massachusetts as the launching point for her rock career. Tracy is a classically trained violinist and pianist but

CHAPTER 10 - 1995-1996: CAPITALIZING ON IT ALL

while attending the Berklee College of Music in Boston beginning in 1987, Bonham describes how she felt about her adopted hometown.

"Boston, at that time, '87, '88, '89, was so vibrant. I started to tap into that scene and once I did, it blew my mind. I had already been listening to bands like the Pixies and I was really interested in the fire and spirit of that music. Coming from a classical upbringing, I wanted more fire. I loved classical music, and still do, and I love that I have it as a musical foundation. But I was looking for that fire and passion of something different. I was always a bit of a rebel too so thumbing my nose at my upbringing was adding to the energy and passion I was now involved with."

What I love about Tracy's description of where her mind and soul were during this time is that so many of the musicians I spoke with or those I've read about in other interviews, all have similar takes on what lured them into making music based on feel, need, passion, and fire. People who didn't know one another, or their music, but somehow wanted the same thing. The beginnings of the alternative and grunge movements were so organic, backed up by the words of Tracy and others who came on the scene back then.

Tracy continued, "It all opened my mind so much that as I started writing songs around that time, I recognized how pure and simple they were. Classically trained Tracy wasn't writing them because I wanted to go away from that side and explore the power behind pure simplicity and power."

We would continue our discussion about this because it fascinated me that a musician with so much classical training and spot-on musical theory behind her could find the thrill of making music not based strictly on those principles. Tracy discussed what would ultimately attract her to this style and it was powerful. As she would see and become inspired by local bands in Boston at that time, she said, "It wasn't really about talent, it was whether or not I believed them."

That resonated strongly with me. It's not to say that these underground artists, some of whom would become history-making musicians down the road, weren't talented, not even close. But what was more important was how genuine and how all-in these bands were. Could we believe them? I feel the same way as a fan, so I knew exactly what Tracy was talking about.

1995 was the year that I was supposed to graduate from college, thrusting me into a world I knew I was ill-prepared for. A curveball was thrown my way however, well it was actually a basketball, and this would delay my graduation to 1996. I was playing in a basketball league and one night during practice, I tore the ACL in my left knee and would go on to have surgery. We didn't have Google Classroom or Zoom in the 1990s and since I couldn't walk or drive for many weeks before and after having surgery, I couldn't get to school to finish my senior year on time. This was a pivotal time for me as I was forced to be alone with my thoughts with very little interaction from the outside world. With no cell phones or social media to speak of, I once again turned to music to keep me company. Unfortunately, even that couldn't keep the demons once again creeping in at bay.

My knee injury occurred in April of '95 and just a month prior, one of the more influential bands of the era, Faith No More had released its fifth studio album, *King for a Day . . . Fool for a Lifetime*. Formed in 1979, in San Francisco, California, under the names Sharp Young Men and Faith No Man before permanently switching to Faith No More in September of 1983, Faith No More has always been ahead of the curve when it comes to their sound. Influences as varied as noise rock, rap, metal, thrash, and hardcore punk, FNM is viewed by critics, artists, and fans alike as one of the most influential bands of its time. The band's breakthrough album, 1989's *The Real Thing*, catapulted them to commercial success and superstardom due mainly to its crossover single (and video) "Epic."

With riff-heavy, metal-influenced music, paired with the powerful, rap-style vocals of singer Mike Patton, "Epic" helped bridge the gap between rock and rap music (successfully done first with the release of "Walk This Way" by

CHAPTER 10 – 1995-1996: CAPITALIZING ON IT ALL

Run-D.M.C. and Aerosmith in 1986), which eventually influenced bands like Rage Against The Machine, Incubus, Korn, Linkin Park, and others in what would become known as the rap/metal and Nu-metal genres. I bring up their history and influence because I was already a huge fan of FNM dating back to the late '80s and by the time *King for a Day . . . Fool for a Lifetime* was released; it had quickly become one of my favorite albums of the '90s and '95 was still barely underway. This record kept me company while I rotted away on my mother's couch as I waited for my knee to heal. As great as the record was and as much as I was looking forward to walking again and eventually graduating from college, something wasn't right.

As I've mentioned, I was prone to depression dating back to eight or nine years old when I first told my mom that I no longer wanted to be alive. I saw a therapist for the first time at nine years old and it seemed as though I was gearing up for needing to see one again. I'm not sure if I was nervous about graduation with no idea what I wanted to do as far as a career was concerned or perhaps, I was feeling sorry for myself about my injured knee, but I was heading down a dark path that would quickly get worse. Being someone who saw every glass as half empty and having already experienced depression and anxiety as a kid, I felt it all coming on. The fear of the future was real.

My parents were both city workers with decent job security and pensions. They never really seemed happy with their work though and I wasn't interested in following in those footsteps. Truth be told, I didn't even want to go to college in the first place. I wanted to somehow be involved in the world of music and that's all I'd ever thought I'd do. I had no clue as to what type of job or how I would even get one, and I didn't have anything remotely close to a plan that would lead me in that direction. I felt rudderless and no one was there to captain my ship. I wasn't like most of my friends, my parents, or other adults I knew who wanted to become civil servants. I wasn't interested in Wall Street or business of any kind. I didn't fit in anywhere and I started feeling like it was once again time to check out.

ROB JANICKE

I may have been feeling unsettled inside my head, but the world around me was just as unsettling. I truly believe that the cultural strife discussed throughout the book thus far, and a few more examples I'll give before you finish reading, overlooked contributing factors to why so much great and diverse music was coming out during the 1990s. The constant air of anger, depression, and confusion that Gen X kids were living through needed an outlet. Music became the biggest outlet available to them. A great number of artists also fell under Generation X, so they understood what the fans were dealing with. They say timing is everything and in the case of the grunge and alternative music that was dominating the globe at this time, a truer statement couldn't be found.

On October 3, 1995, the world would finally know the outcome of the trial of the century. The fate of O.J. Simpson will be revealed. After an 11-month trial, it took the jury only four hours of deliberation to come up with a "not guilty" verdict, leading to more anger and confusion that had already surrounded this case. To date, the murders of Nicole Brown Simpson and Ron Goldman remain unsolved.

Earlier that year, the country, along with my generation, witnessed a very violent and unexpected display of domestic terrorism. At 9:02 AM on April 19th, a truck full of explosives was detonated outside a United States federal government complex in downtown Oklahoma City, Oklahoma. The explosives were a mixture of diesel, ammonium nitrate fertilizer, and nitromethane which had been packed into 13 barrels within the truck, weighing a total of 4,800 pounds.

The targeted building, the Alfred P. Murrah Federal Building, partially collapsed within seven seconds of the detonation, leaving the building structurally unstable. The blast destroyed nearly everything within a 16-block radius of the intended target, demolishing or damaging 324 nearby buildings, burning 86 cars, and causing an estimated 652 million dollars in damages. The attack took the lives of 168 people while injuring

CHAPTER 10 – 1995-1996: CAPITALIZING ON IT ALL

an additional 680. The VIN number found on the axle of the exploded truck was used to trace it back to Timothy McVeigh, a former U.S. soldier, who was arrested the same day for driving without a valid license plate and carrying an unlicensed weapon. McVeigh had an accomplice, former Army roommate, Terry Nichols, who were both now anti-government and white supremacist extremists, looking to further their propaganda by inflicting the most damage possible.

On June 2, 1997, McVeigh was found guilty of using a weapon of mass destruction, while Nichols stood trial twice and was ultimately found guilty of 161 counts of murder for his role in the domestic terror plot and execution. On June 11, 2001, McVeigh was put to death by lethal injection making him the first federally executed person in 38 years. Terry Nichols is currently serving 161 consecutive life sentences with no possibility of parole.

Grunge and alternative music up until this point in the '90s was associated with heavy guitar riffs with drop D tuning, bass grooves that moved the songs along, and lyrics about depression, anger, boredom, addiction, and isolation. There were other sounds and topics to be found throughout the scene, but commercially speaking, this is what the movement was becoming known for.

A very important record that would challenge that perception in 1995 was the third studio album by the Chicago band Smashing Pumpkins called *Mellon Collie and the Infinite Sadness*. As mentioned earlier, the Pumpkins first appeared on the scene in 1991 with their outstanding debut album, *Gish*, linking them with the other iconic releases of that historic year. Following *Gish* was the 1993 release, *Siamese Dream* which blew up and ultimately sold over six million copies, forever cementing The Smashing Pumpkins as one of the best-selling and most influential bands of the era. With all that success though, it's my opinion that the 1995 release of *Mellon Collie . . .* was the band's defining moment to this very day.

ROB JANICKE

A double album, much more of a '70s thing than a '90s one, *Mellon Collie and the Infinite Sadness* had all the elements of what you'd expect from an alternative/grunge band of the time but lead singer and songwriter Billy Corgan wove something quite different over this record. Along with the big riffs and blaring drums, Corgan wrote and arranged orchestral pieces and very delicate songs throughout the album. With 28 tracks on two CDs or three vinyl records, listening to *Mellon Collie* needed your time and undivided attention to take it all in. The record begins with a beautiful instrumental track, with melody and hooks throughout.

Unlike what was popular at the time, the song didn't consist of distorted guitars but instead, classical string instruments you'd hear on something recorded centuries before. This was Corgan's way of letting us know we'd be in for a sonic journey with many surprise roads and rivers to cross. The band delivered that message as I believe this record was one of the most unique and creative records to have come out of the entire decade and even with all the attention it garnered, it still doesn't get the respect it deserves.

This record proved, at least on a commercial level, that softer music, played with real emotion, can have just as big an impact on fans of grunge and alternative music as the heavier stuff had when the scene first blew up. It's always been my contention that one of the biggest reasons this music resonated with so many people (and still does) had more to do with the honesty and vulnerability of the lyrics and the topics that were being written about, more so than the sound of the music alone. The combination of the words, subject matter, and music though, was what put this scene over the top and it's why so many of us who were teenagers at the time can still identify with it today. In my mind, *Mellon Collie and the Infinite Sadness* was the album that brought it all together.

Rising from the ashes of Nirvana's demise due to the sudden death of Kurt Cobain, a new "band" arose featuring the band's drummer, Dave

CHAPTER 10 – 1995-1996: CAPITALIZING ON IT ALL

Grohl called Foo Fighters. I chose to put quotations around the word band because at this stage, the "band" consisted of only one member, Dave Grohl. The self-titled album was released on July 4, 1995, and it was written and recorded by Grohl himself. He wrote all the music and lyrics and played all the instruments. There was one slight exception, Greg Duli of the band Afghan Whigs, added some guitar work to the album's 10th track, "X-Static."

Other than that, this was the Dave Grohl show. Grohl had stated many times that this "band" was initially created as a project to help him deal with the loss of his friend and Nirvana bandmate, Kurt Cobain, with no expectations other than releasing the songs as a demo. Things changed quickly however and the collection of songs that would become *Foo Fighters* were professionally produced by Grohl and Barrett Jones in Seattle and ultimately released by Roswell and Capital Records. Foo Fighters would later become an actual band, although Grohl would remain the band's songwriter, by adding touring and recording musicians, including ex-Nirvana bandmate, and punk legend, Pat Smear on guitar.

Foo Fighters have been and currently are one of the biggest rock bands in the world, basically dating back to their second record in 1997, *The Colour and the Shape*. With album sales being a bit of a mystery once digital music took over, estimates are varied but no one can argue that Dave Grohl is one of the most popular and best-selling artists of all time. It is estimated that Nirvana has sold over 75 million records worldwide and Foo Fighters have sold over 32 million and counting. Being a part of one of the most commercially successful and culturally impactful bands in the history of music is nearly impossible. Dave Grohl has done it twice!

In sticking with the theme of doing something twice, 1995 was the year the second-largest live music phenomenon of the '90s made its debut. Like Lollapalooza before it (1991), The Warped Tour (officially changed its name to The Vans Warped Tour the following year when the shoe company joined as the title sponsor), a traveling punk rock festival that not only embraced music but also the DIY ethos of the underground and the skateboarding culture that was tremendously popular amongst teenagers during the 1990s.

Conceived by Kevin Lyman, live music and event aficionado (Kevin was the first stage manager for Lollapalooza since that tour's inception), and Ray Woodbury, president of RK Diversified Entertainment, the tour kicked off on June 21, 1995, in Boise, Idaho and has gone on to become North Americas longest running music festival to date. Not only did The Warped Tour shine a bright light on the punk alternative music of the day, by helping bands such as NOFX, Fishbone, The Mighty Mighty Bosstones, Pennywise, Social Distortion, Deftones, Rancid, Bad Religion, and so many others reach huge audiences (the tour attracted about 750,000 people annually), it also highlighted charitable and not for profit causes.

Organizations such as Invisible Children, Keep A Breast Foundation, Hope For The Day, and Music Saves Lives, among others, were given a platform that they likely would not have been able to create on their own. Lyman and company took their love of music, and positive attitude toward bands and audiences and brought millions of people together through the love and power of music.

Our friend from earlier in the book, Eileen Mercolino, was also a part of The Vans Warped Tour as she was hired in 1996 to help guide and build it to what it eventually became. There's something to be said for having some insight into something massive that started with a whisper. Looking back on those early days of the tour, Mercolino said, "We had so much fun back then. It was like traveling with your best friends and family, sharing BBQ food and music, and figuring it all out along the way. In those early days, the tour was held together with zip ties and duct tape. It was wild." As a quick aside, Mercolino would certainly understand the chaos and

CHAPTER 10 - 1995-1996: CAPITALIZING ON IT ALL

wildness of the music industry by this time as already referenced with her work with Mother Love Bone and Pearl Jam, but Eileen also worked for acclaimed music manager, John Silva (Nirvana, Beck, Foo Fighters, Beastie Boys, NIN, Norah Jones, etc.) and here's the kicker . . . she was hired the same day Kurt Cobain's body was found. Talk about being thrown into the fire!

As things tend to do in society, the longer something is in vogue, the closer it gets to cultural extinction. 1996 would mark the fifth year grunge and alternative music called the shots commercially and artistically for the youth of America and across the globe. Of course, pop music never went away, nor did country music, as those genres are timeless and never quite leave the eyes and ears of popular culture. Grunge, alternative, punk, and hip-hop, however, had taken a significant stranglehold over Generation X, and with a few years still to go before the decade would come to its end, this was still the case. There were some signs though that where grunge, punk, and alternative were at the top of the musical food chain, hip-hop was about to start spreading its wings wider than ever before. This was also the year where technology, not quite as we know it today of course, began to creep ever so slightly into our daily lives. Technology, not genres of music, would ultimately change the music industry, and the world, upside down soon enough.

With Kurt Cobain's death being almost two years old by '96, there were some cracks in the overall foundation of grunge beginning to show. Don't get me wrong, you wouldn't have bet on it all going away anytime soon back in 1996, but if you were paying close enough attention, things were shifting just a little bit. Some of the mainstays of the grunge and alternative movement released albums in 1996 but they didn't have the impact previous releases of theirs once had. Albums such as *No Code* (Pearl Jam), *Down on the Upside* (Soundgarden), *New Adventures in Hi-Fi*

(R.E.M.), and *Load* (Metallica) were released to mixed reviews by fans and critics alike, and in the case of *Load*, fans were downright angry with the band due to its poor and dare I say, sophomoric production.

Some records by the bigger bands of the decade, however, did meet or exceed expectations. All was not lost for the scene but there was a noticeable shift in what people were interested in listening to. *Evil Empire* (Rage Against the Machine), *MTV Unplugged* (Alice In Chains), and *Tiny Music . . . Songs from the Vatican Gift Shop* (Stone Temple Pilots) were all released to positive reviews and for those fanbases, it wasn't all that different from what life was like during the first few years of the decade.

1996 was, in my opinion, the beginning of the end of the grunge movement as we had come to know it. Kurt was dead, Alice In Chains lead singer Layne Staley was battling a very difficult heroin addiction as was evident on the band's MTV appearance on Unplugged which aired in May of that year, Pearl Jam would release its most non-commercial album, *No Code*, to date in August of '96 which the band has hinted was done purposely to scale back the attention they were still receiving since its debut in 1991, and Soundgarden's *Down on the Upside* was met with mixed reviews at best. It sold well but didn't move the needle as much as previous releases had.

Coupled with this, we started to see some releases from older bands, not associated with the grunge or alternative scene, put out records that deviated from what those bands were known for, and tried to emulate what was happening in the grunge and alternative world. Once things like that start to happen in a creative scene, it's likely time to move on. The most notable came from 1980s rock giants, Def Leppard with their release of *Slang*. In an interview with Ken McIntyre of Classic Rock Magazine, Def Leppard guitarist Vivian Campbell said this about the direction and sound of *Slang*:

"We knew we couldn't make a typical Def Leppard album in the mid-

CHAPTER 10 – 1995-1996: CAPITALIZING ON IT ALL

1990s. Grunge was very much happening, and our stuff was anathema at the time . . . Personally, I think we could have bolstered the songs with a little more of that Def Lep fairy dust . . . but instead, we went, 'No, let's keep it raw: no backing vocals; let's not do that part because it's too melodic; let's be more monotone . . . At least it gave us the chance to grow up a little. We live in a state of arrested development in this band, singing songs like '*Let's Get Rocked.*' So, we did get to write some grown-up lyrics. And we were going through a lot of shit at that time: Sav's dad died on the eve of the first recording day; both Joe and Phil were going through divorces . . . So, it gave us an opportunity to write lyrics that reflected the reality of our lives."

In addition to older bands trying to sound new, new (or new-ish) bands were making important records that were sounding a bit different from what the early '90s had given us. I will always contend that had it not been for the popularity and impact of that early grunge and alternative scene, much of the new music that came out in the mid to late '90s wouldn't have been accepted by the masses, so the influence was real, but the sound was starting to wane. Albums like *Antichrist Superstar* (Marilyn Manson), *Tidal* (Fiona Apple), *Sublime* (Sublime), *Odelay* (Beck), and *Among My Swan* (Mazzy Star) were creatively, sonically, and visually giving us something we really hadn't seen commercially before this time. There were also "pop" versions of what was being called alternative at this time that had begun to rule both the radio and MTV airwaves. Albums such as *Crash* (Dave Matthews Band), *Yourself or Someone Like You* (Matchbox Twenty), *Sheryl Crow* (Sheryl Crow), and *Bringing Down the Horse* (The Wallflowers) were becoming household names. These albums were a far cry from the dark-sounding and bleak subject matter from what came from the earlier part of the decade. I think people were sick of feeling sick and sad and needed something with much less weight attached to it.

The biggest sign that things were changing however was the start of the "Boy/Girl Band" movement. 1996 would see the debut albums of both the Spice Girls and Backstreet Boys with the releases of *Spice* and *Backstreet Boys* respectively. I'm not the person to write intelligently about either band but I can tell you that the global influence and popularity of both bands would change the musical landscape going forward. Another important change in music that would wind up affecting culture right through to today was the creative force that hip-hop was becoming.

Rap music, as we called it in the '80s, had rebranded itself as hip-hop along the way, and its relevance and influence on music, culture, and society, is not up for debate. My children are both in grammar school as this book is being written (I have two kids, 10 and 7 years old) and hip-hop music and culture are most of what they're interested in, as are most of their friends. Back in the 1980s when stuffy, old white men were claiming rap wasn't "real" music and it was just a fad that would soon go away, myself and others who were blown away by these new sounds instinctively knew these naysayers were fools motivated by racist ideals and we shunned all their opinions on the matter. Turns out, we were right! As we speak, hip-hop is in the middle of celebrating its 50th anniversary, and in some ways, it feels like it's just getting started.

Hip-hop was already huge by the mid-'90s but a few records that were released in '96 stick out more than others. *The Score* (Fugees), *Reasonable Doubt* (Jay-Z), *It Was Written* (Nas), and *All Eyez on Me* (Tupac Shakur) due to their musical and cultural significance. Other hip-hop albums released that year saw the debut of Lil' Kim with *Hardcore*, Foxy Brown with *Ill Na Na*, and a record that almost no one bought by an artist who would soon dominate the entire genre, *Infinite* by Eminem. Hip-hop was here and here to stay. 1996 played a massive role in hip-hop's foundation and legacy.

The '90s were a very diverse and experimental time concerning the

CHAPTER 10 - 1995-1996: CAPITALIZING ON IT ALL

music that was coming out. This is one of the reasons I'm not a fan of labeling music but instead, see it as a necessary evil when writing about it or trying to have a conversation with people about the music you want to discuss. Hip-hop was reaching a fever pitch in the mid-'90s yet the type of hip-hop that we were hearing was so varied that the term "hip-hop" wasn't enough to describe it. A good example of this would be the crossover hip-hop band, Arrested Development, discussed a bit earlier in the book. Dubbed "alternative hip-hop," AD's style, sound, and message were an alternative to gangsta rap which was the dominant style of hip-hop in the late '80s and early '90s, due mainly to the success of L.A.'s N.W.A.

Arrested Development played a very significant role in alternative music of all kinds in the early '90s as I believe they were one of the hip-hop bands that were able to speak to fans of all musical leanings. Their music, production, and lyrical content were not only top-notch, but the timing of their message and popularity fit in perfectly with what was happening in the alternative and grunge rock world at the time. The band offered a positive balance from the heaviness of the Seattle scene, and they allowed people who may not have necessarily been fans of rap music yet to experience a different type of musicianship than what they might have been hearing from the genre at the time. The band was all over the radio and MTV with hits such as, "Mr. Wendal," "Everyday People," and "Tennessee." The album was voted "Best Album of the Year" by The Village Voice and The Wire. The record was also included in the book, *1001 Albums You Must Hear Before You Die*, and the song "Tennessee" is a part of the *Rock 'n' roll Hall of Fame's 500 Songs that Shaped Rock 'n' roll* list.

In talking with Speech about his take on Lollapalooza earlier and now about Arrested Development's latest release, *For The FKN Love* (as well as the band's legacy), I was able to get a well-round idea of why the band's influence still carries on to this day. With Arrested Development being so different right from its inception, I was curious as to why and how Speech formed his band bucking the hip-hop trends that were popular at the time, and if he thought it would affect his career negatively.

"Ya know for me, I was in some rap groups before Arrested Development and I was doing some Run-DMC sounding stuff and trying to be like Public Enemy, I was trying to be other things because I'm from Milwaukee and we didn't have any successful hip-hop artists there. And if you remember back during that time, hip-hop was primarily East Coast/West Coast. We didn't even have a worldwide scene in the South yet. So, I looked at being different as a plus to help me stand out, not to mention I had finally found myself. So, I didn't want to sound like anyone else and I didn't want to follow the trends per se."

This made sense to me because as a writer (I started writing poetry and song lyrics as early as 15 years old), it's taken me a long time to find my voice. I think most creative endeavors do take some time to fully absorb the will and personality of the people creating the art. I wanted to know about Speech's musical influences as well because his sound is unique, and you can hear different genres of music throughout Arrested Development's catalog.

Speech shared, "In addition to some of the bands I mentioned to you before, I also loved Kraftwerk and Planet Patrol, so there were a lot of different textures that were being created at the start of hip-hop that made it wonderfully diverse."

It's this exact diversity that made Arrested Development fit in so well with the music of the early '90s and in part, has allowed them to be relevant 30-plus years later. The '90s were a very fertile and creative period, especially the early part of the decade, and one of the reasons I wanted to write this book in the first place was to hopefully shine a light on that fact.

CHAPTER 11 – 1997-1998
THE TIMES, THEY ARE A-CHANGIN': WE ARE CONFLICTED

"MUSIC?! WHAT ARE YOU GONNA DO, STAND ON A CORNER IN NEW YORK CITY AND BANG ON A drum? Get a real job!" These are words my dad would say to me the two or three times I'd ever discussed my future with him over the years. I was only out of college for about a year or so between '97 and '98 when I heard those words of wisdom for the last time. Let's just say I didn't experience a ton of encouragement when it came to the things I wanted to do. I don't remember what response, if any, I had to that sage advice, but it made enough of an impression to write about it all these years later.

That was the generation of most adults back in the '90s it seemed. I can remember a very specific interaction with the woman who hired me for the "real" job (it was in NYC, and I had to wear a tie and everything! Woo-hoo, I'd made it!) I had right out of school. "As a kid, if you were told you could have any job in the world, call it your dream job if you will, what would it be?" said Barbara, the HR manager who hired me.

I thought for what seemed like 5 minutes, mainly because I thought it was a dumb question. I certainly was not going to say that it was the job I was there to interview for, so instead, I was honest. My reply was, "It would either be to play shortstop for the New York Yankees or play bass guitar for

Iron Maiden. Unfortunately, I could never play as fast as Steve Harris does, and the Yankees seem all set at SS with that kid, Derek Jeter." Barbara went on to call me a "dreamer," a nice way of saying, "pick a real job," but liked my honest and creative answer. I was hired. Call me crazy, but this was not a good day for me. Road to misery, here I come.

When you write a letter to your parents about how your life isn't worth living at 24 years old, and how you can't find purpose or happiness in anything you do, it's a solid bet you've got some demons you cannot conquer on your own. I must've written that letter 25 times before settling on the final draft. Once I was satisfied it contained all the brilliant points and reasons I had laid out as to why I was feeling the way I was, I sealed it, put it in a safe place, and waited for the right time to send it.

1991 felt like a lifetime ago as the late '90s were upon us. Some of the early grunge and alternative music was starting to already feel like classic rock to some of us while hip-hop, nu-metal country, bubblegum pop, Brit-pop, and grunge imitators were dominating music and culture. As discussed throughout the book, the world during the decade of the '90s was a weird, at times violent, and usually confusing place. Music is what identified the times more than anything and typically brought people together for positive reasons. Even the negativity that was on display during the decade had provided a creative spark that was absolutely behind some of the best and most culturally significant music the world had seen in a very long time. 1997 wasn't lacking in the "why is this decade so screwed up" department.

In February of that year, O.J. Simpson was found liable for the deaths of his ex-wife, Nicole Brown Simpson, and Ron Goldman in a civil court action. Just another reason to be angered and confused. Did he or did he not commit those murders? Most believe he did. One trial says no, the other says yes, and the circus never wants to leave town. Although we already had a religious cult-led tragedy in Waco, Texas, why not have another for good measure? This time I'm referring to the Heaven's Gate cult. On March 26,

CHAPTER 11 - 1997-1998: THE TIMES, THEY ARE A-CHANGIN'

1997, 39 bodies were discovered inside a house in San Diego, California wearing black tracksuits, and sneakers, and having consumed apple sauce laced with barbiturates.

In the eyes of the cult, this was not a mass suicide but rather the preparation needed to free their souls to board a spaceship that would deliver them to their new homes in outer space. Bags were placed over their heads, and purple garments were covering their bodies. This was a mass suicide, none of what the cult believed in was based in any form of reality, and these poor people had nothing to show for it but pictures of their corpses and their ever-present, Nike sneakers. Add to this the mysterious car accident resulting in the death of the beloved Princess Diana of Wales and the year has more than its share of very high-profile and disturbing cultural events.

Where there are downs, however, there also tend to be ups. Some very interesting events that would not only acknowledge how closely connected culture and music are, 1997 would slowly but surely usher in the digital age we live in today. It's difficult to find an argument that says The Beatles aren't the most or one of the most famous and influential bands of all time. Even if you're not as enamored with them musically as so many are, denying that their music has changed the world since they landed in New York in February of 1964 would have you come across as foolish and honestly, wrong.

On March 11, 1997, Queen Elizabeth II knighted Paul McCartney, forever changing his name to Sir Paul McCartney. This is a goodwill gesture and recognition of Paul's contribution to music and culture with The Beatles and beyond, and not something that holds any weight in any political or governance sense. It does however show the indelible connection certain music and musicians can have on the world thus strengthening the bond between artist, scene, and fan. The fact that the knighthood of one of the most recognizable figures in music over the last 60-plus years took place in the '90s was just another small way the universe was telling us that the '90s would hold an extremely significant place in the history of music.

Music wasn't the only artistic medium to inform culture in the 1990s. MTV was the logical go-to for the combination of music and television during the '90s, but both network and cable TV stations were creating the culture and society-defining programming that would live on in infamy. Shows such as *The Simpsons* and *Seinfeld* (despite debuting in 1989) would dominate television audiences everywhere throughout the '90s and change how TV (and what can be successful on TV) is programmed and watched forever.

A show that debuted in 1997, however, was more in line with the attitude, angst, sarcasm, and frustration of its generation and target audience more than any other. With its first episode airing on August 13, 1997, *South Park*, created by Trey Parker and Matt Stone, began its assault on everyone and everything in its way. There wasn't a topic, a person or group of people, religion, political affiliation, musical style, institution, tradition, or anything else you can think of that was exempt from its cartoon anti-heroes to destroy. I fell in love with the series immediately and likened it to a new, animated, version of *All in the Family*, the 1970s sitcom created by Norman Lear which introduced the world to Archie Bunker, an ignorant bigot with likeable qualities.

South Park captured the world in the exact moment it was in and anyone who was being honest with themselves (then or now) should be able to see a little of themselves in this series. Good, bad, or otherwise, we're a flawed race and sometimes it takes other people and perspectives to show us how much more improvement we truly need. I applaud Parker and Stone for having the guts, humor, brains, and vision to put this out. As I write this, the series has completed its 26th season of being on the air. This series, as is much of the music of the decade, is another example of how influential the '90s were both creatively and culturally. So much of what happened back then changed the lives of millions and created enough drive and passion to create their life's work from what they witnessed (or learned about afterward) so many years ago.

CHAPTER 11 - 1997-1998: THE TIMES, THEY ARE A-CHANGIN'

Television and music ruled the entertainment day back then, but 1997 saw an event that went under the radar yet had global and historical ramifications no one knew about at the time. On September 15, the website google.com was registered as a domain name. The internet was a miniscule shell of what it would one day become in 1997, but this seemingly insignificant registration would soon turn the world upside down.

I would surmise that 1997 is the year that many people who are my age and were fans of the music coming out of Seattle in the late '80s/early '90s, would say that grunge had finally died. This is subjective, and a music scene can never die if there are still people writing and playing it and fans listening to and buying it, but from a cultural standpoint, scenes do come to an end. I use 1997 for many reasons but the one that seems to have always stood out for me in having this opinion is the fact that 1997 is the year that Soundgarden broke up. Since then, the band would reunite, record new music, and tour until the untimely death of lead singer and main songwriter, Chris Cornell at the age of 52, when he committed suicide in his Detroit hotel room after performing with Soundgarden earlier that evening. At the time though, no one could know any of this would happen and as it turned out, the band wouldn't reunite for 13 years, so 1997 seemed like the end. In retrospect, perhaps it should have been.

Soundgarden's importance to the movement that was grunge, and the early '90s Seattle scene, simply cannot be heralded enough. I spoke about them earlier in the book as the band formed back in 1984 and was truly one of the pioneers of the entire movement. There have been books written about the band and on Cornell alone because that's just how influential and important they were to music and culture over the last 40 years. Hell, even Kristina Marie, former MTV segment producer and interviewed throughout the book, once tricked an intern at the music television giant to switch assignments with her all so she could interview Chris Cornell. Everyone knew the importance of this band.

On April 9, 1997, the band announced its decision to disband, thus in my eyes, ending the run of dominance by the Seattle music scene, grunge, alternative, or whatever you'd like to call it, for good. What seemed like the blink of an eye from 1991-1997 was now a moment in time, ready to move aside for what was next. What was next was big, and branches from this tree only grew wider and longer, but the initial seed, that first bloom if you will, had withered. It was time.

Good rock music was still coming out in 1997, but its relevance was minimal compared to what it had been just a few short years earlier. Records like Faith No More's *Album of the Year*, David Bowie's *Earthling*, *Nimrod* by Green Day, *Lovesongs for Underdogs* by Tanya Donelly, *Dig Me Out* by Sleeter Kinney, and *The Colour and the Shape* by Foo Fighters are just a few that still brought excitement to what was fast becoming the old guard of '90s music fans. Part of the reason you know a scene is ending though, is when the bands that were viewed as frauds, bandwagoners, and parody acts by an overwhelming majority of people who were there when the grunge and alternative scene first took hold in 1991, began to top the charts. Debut albums by Creed (*My Own Prison*), Third Eye Blind (*Third Eye Blind*), and Days of the New (*Days of the New*) started to dominate alternative radio and MTV, commercially signaling the end of an era. Luckily though, hip-hop was continuing its surge in societal viability with albums by Jay-Z (*In My Lifetime, Vol. 1*), Wu-Tang Clan (*Wu-Tang Forever*), and Life After Death (*The Notorious B.I.G.*), thus keeping alive the creativity and relevance of what was now a not-so-new genre but one of the biggest musical and cultural forces in the world.

Having finally graduated from college, the world was looking scarier by the day. I still wanted nothing but to make my life's work all about music but was increasingly becoming despondent around the fact that I had no idea how to do such a thing. I was still living in my mom's house in Brooklyn and commuting into Manhattan every day for my job as a sales assistant at a large communications company. I worked for a Television Rep firm selling airtime

CHAPTER 11 - 1997-1998: THE TIMES, THEY ARE A-CHANGIN'

to network TV affiliates around the country. Exciting, I know. It was your basic, entry-level data entry sales job. I had to input sales orders and speak with television station workers across the land on the phone all day long. This was my first (and unfortunately not my last) tussle with corporate America. I say it that way because the corporate environment never, not once, felt right to me. I'm not built for it, and I knew that from the very beginning.

Most of my former co-workers, managers, employers, and customers would agree. I ask too many questions, don't know how to stop talking when I should, am not much of a conformist, and generally don't enjoy doing what I'm told to do by anyone. If you're guessing that my attitude, personality, and mental state of being around this time were less than stellar, you'd be correct. I broke a lot of rules while working at this job (as well as the ones I'd have in the future). This isn't something I'm bragging about or proud of, quite the opposite. I was mortified and angry about so many of the things I did and the places I agreed to work. Not because of the people I worked with (a few exceptions notwithstanding of course), but because I knew in my soul, I didn't belong. I didn't know how to break the cycle. This is a feeling I've been all too familiar with throughout my life.

Since the age of five, when my parents got divorced, dealing with some traumatic events from around the ages of 9-11 and wanting to die, I never felt like I fit in. I never truly pursued what I wanted for fear of not living up to the expectations of others. I faked it all well enough though. I bet some people are reading this right now who had no idea I felt anything like this, but I did. I may not have been great at finding happiness for myself, but I was great at making anyone believe that I was. Looking back at it now, and honestly, knowing then, lying to myself was a very dark and lonely place to be. I don't know how close I was to doing what I asserted I should in that letter to my parents, hell, I hadn't even sent it to them yet. But I was very, very far from being ok.

When we as music fans hear the term, "That's their Sgt. Pepper's," we all know what it means. For those of you who may not understand the saying, it means that when referring to a band's best album or any album that was a massive success culturally, commercially, and artistically, we are saying it's their "Sgt. Pepper's" to compare it to what some feel is the greatest and most important record of all time, the 1967 release by The Beatles, *Sgt. Pepper's Lonely Hearts Club Band*. The term can get overused and sometimes used incorrectly. In the case of one album that came out in 1997 though, the phrase is right on the money. It's a bullseye.

Released on May 21, 1997, *OK Computer* by the British band Radiohead, marked a sea change in popular music. Already having two previous records out and a modest following, especially after the group's second album, *The Bends* came out in 1995 to favorable reviews, the band and its record label EMI, had higher hopes for its third effort. No one saw the tsunami of praise about to crash onto the band, especially those following the successful Britpop scene of the '90s (which included some bands that started many years before the '90s) including heavyweights such as Oasis, Pulp, Blur, The Stone Roses, James, Elastica, and so on. *OK Computer* changed the way critics, fans, and musicians alike heard music at this point and the decade took a dramatic turn from anything that had come before it.

When I first heard this album, having already been a marginal fan of the band's previous releases, I knew my generation's Sgt. Pepper's had landed. For the timing, catchiness, aggression, and sound that was Nirvana's Nevermind six years earlier, *OK Computer* was a landscape of sonic atmosphere that seeped into your bloodstream, ultimately finding a spot in your soul. I didn't completely understand it musically, because of its experimentalism, complex arrangements, unabashed genuineness, and artistic vulnerability, but I knew I loved it and would for the rest of time. Its impact was that great. *OK Computer* effectively ended the prior Britpop movement putting a larger emphasis on more atmospheric, guitar-driven, progressive rock with dark and intro-

CHAPTER 11 - 1997-1998: THE TIMES, THEY ARE A-CHANGIN'

spective undertones. The album has been cited in most respected publications "Best Albums of All Time" lists including NME, Melody Maker, Alternative Press, Pitchfork, Spin, Time, and Rolling Stone to name a few.

With an album as successful as *OK Computer*, there are bound to be detractors and this record was no exception. To date, estimates have Radiohead's album sales at over 30 million with *OK Computer* accounting for over seven million of those records. These types of numbers bring the naysayers out sometimes. In a poll conducted by BBC Radio 6 Music, *OK Computer* was voted the sixth most overrated album of all time. David H. Green of Britain's The Daily Telegraph had this to say about Radiohead's most famous album, "self-indulgent whingeing" while adding, "a 20th-century delusion that rock is the bastion of serious commentary on popular music." It should be noted that I vehemently disagree with both the BBC poll and Mr. Green's findings, but they have the right to their opinions, I guess.

If I could count the times, I felt like music had saved my life, I'd probably still be counting. I can say though, that upon hearing *OK Computer* in 1997, with most of the music I loved seemingly in neutral and not sure when or if it would ever drive forward again, my faith in music had been restored, and although it was slight, I had some hope for the future.

The 1990s had such an odd collection of cultural events that as the decade was ending, I think our society had become either numb to certain behaviors or in some cases, simply didn't care. For my generation I think most of us felt one of those two ways when it came to what was probably the biggest distraction infecting our culture, the Bill Clinton/Monica Lewinsky scandal. In January of 1998, the world learned of a rumored affair involving United States President Bill Clinton and White House intern, Monica Lewinsky. As speculation and details emerged, the world would learn that an affair had happened and dated back to 1995 when the President was 49 and Lewinsky was 22. The relationship lasted for 18 months, ending in 1997. Some of the music that was railing against government, political figures, and just about any other form of bullshit, status quo life during the '90s, may have been gone, but it was par for the course that the decade was coming close to its end with these types of shenanigans taking place.

Seemingly ignoring or vowing to do the opposite of what was happening in society during the '90s by people other than Gen Xers, young people were still very much engaged in creating a future for themselves in which humanity, caring, and fairness would be the framework of their purpose with music being the common denominator that brings it all together. Part of what made the music from the early '90s so special, particularly the grunge movement, was the inclusivity shown from artist to fan. This dates to the punk rock ethos of the mid to late '70s when punk bands didn't want to play on stages to not appear "above" their fans. It was supposed to be about community and equality. It sounds unattainable to some, and it didn't always play out in kind. But most bands who stood by that ethos tried very hard to live that way as much as possible while balancing a career in the spotlight.

One of the original Seattle bands to make a global impact on the music of the '90s was Pearl Jam. I've discussed them at various points throughout the book because their history and legacy are still being written more than three decades after they released their first record. Some members of the band, Matt Cameron, Stone Gossard, and Jeff Ament, to be specific, have roots in the earliest days of the scene dating back to 1984. I use them as an example here because, from their inception as a group, they have proven time and time again to put their fans first in every way that it's possible for a band of their fame and relevance to do so.

Remember, when they began in 1991, fans and artists had no realistic way of communicating with one another. Outside of TV or print interviews/articles, there wasn't any contact to be had. It's not like today with technology, social media, and a music industry dependent upon regular fan interaction. Bands and fans alike had to make a real effort to try and interact and Pearl Jam made every effort to connect.

"I just wanted to have a party and hang out with these people," said Laura

CHAPTER 11 - 1997-1998: THE TIMES, THEY ARE A-CHANGIN'

DeMartini, President of The Wishlist Foundation, a Pearl Jam fan-run nonprofit, grassroots 501(c)(3) fan organization dedicated to supporting Pearl Jam's charitable and philanthropic efforts. "We are 100% fan-run, independent of the band, its management, or the Ten Club," said DeMartini. Conceived in 2004 and officially organized in 2006, the foundation, through the devotion of Pearl Jam's fan base, has raised over 1.6 million dollars via pre-concert parties, raffles, auctions, and donation gifting.

Laura is one of the founders of the foundation, a lifelong Pearl Jam fan, and a native New Yorker (like me) so finally getting the chance to speak with her after decades of knowing her name and all she's been responsible for was a thrill. I assumed, as I typically do with fans of the early Seattle rock scene, that Laura's introduction to that music was like mine. I wasn't that far off.

"My best friend was working at a record store around the time both *Ten* and *Nevermind* were released (fall of 1991). One day I went to the store to visit her and as I walked in, they had just started playing *Ten* and I was like, wow, what is *this*? It was the instrumental intro to the album, *'Master/Slave'* and it was like nothing else I had ever heard. I was into all the hair bands at the time and hearing those ominous, cool sounds, I was just blown away. As that gave way to the beginning of *'Once'*, I thought, oh shit, I have to buy this," Laura explained then hummed the riff.

Hearing music that connects directly to your soul is a rare yet wonderful experience. I've had it happen a handful of times, hearing *Ten* for the first time, just like Laura, was one of the most significant. That feeling tends to stay with you forever. Laura described that feeling by saying, "It's as if someone blew one of those dog whistles that no one else but you can hear, so you pick up your head, turn toward the sound, and run. It's a calling."

When a band, a musician, a genre, or a scene can have such an effect on one's life that one wants to dedicate a large chunk of their life to it, you know you're existing in rarified air. I wanted to know where the idea for The Wishlist Foundation came from and how it's lasted (and grown) since 2004.

"When the Pearl Jam message boards were at the height of their prosperity, I was a young mom who stayed home to raise my daughter as well as an entrepreneur, juggling my businesses," said Laura. "Although I've always been outgoing," she continued.

"My life at the time sort of dictated that most of my relationships be online. Due to those circumstances, I found a huge community through the Pearl Jam Message Pit. When the band announced their Vote for Change Tour in 2004, a bunch of us online had been talking about arranging a get-together. We all shared a love and admiration for the band, I just wanted to have a party and hang out with these people. It was also around this time that Mike McCready had disclosed that he suffered from Crohn's disease. One of my friends on the board also has Crohn's and since Mike had been so courageous in talking about such a devastatingly personal affliction, he said why don't we take this idea of a party and make it a fundraiser of some sort? We decided to hold a food drive for Pearl Jam's Vote for Change tour stop in St. Louis and ended up with almost 500 pounds of donated food. We were shocked! We said, imagine if we can do this for an entire tour? As people started to see what was happening at that St. Louis show, fans were taking the idea and running with it for the next Pearl Jam tour, which was soon after Vote for Change, across Canada. So, we started organizing pre-show parties and fundraisers for each Canadian stop. By the end of that tour, we had raised over 15 thousand dollars for the Crohn's and Colitis Foundation of Canada in honor of Mike."

With a start like that, how could Laura and the crew not be inspired to continue? Not only did they continue but they did so with absolutely zero involvement from the band. From the initial concept and online discussions in 2004 and the official launch of The Wishlist Foundation in 2006, not a single member of the band (or its management) had been involved. Laura says they had no idea if the band even knew the foundation existed at all.

That changed in 2008, however, when Laura received a call that Mike McCready wanted to meet her and the others responsible for creating and sustaining

CHAPTER 11 - 1997-1998: THE TIMES, THEY ARE A-CHANGIN'

it. Laura and Mike have been friends ever since and have worked on various projects together due to their newfound friendship. Music brings people together folks, and yes, music can change the world. You have to act when it calls. The Wishlist Foundation fundraising and pre-show parties have been just as much a part of Pearl Jam tours as anything else has been since the very first one. Fifty percent of the proceeds go to the band's highlighted charities and the other fifty percent goes to local charities of the city the band is playing in on a particular night.

CHAPTER 12 - 1999
BUBBLEGUM IS BACK: POP MUSIC AND TECHNOLOGY LEFT GRUNGE WITH NOTHING BUT CAVITIES

"BECAUSE OF A BLOWJOB? DOESN'T THE GOVERNMENT HAVE MORE IMPORTANT THINGS TO work on?" I said while discussing the impeachment and eventual acquittal of President Bill Clinton at the start of 1999. The water cooler talk at work during this time was nothing but conversations about a blue dress, sex in the White House, and corruption inside the government. "He's a liar and a cheat and they're doing the right thing by trying to get rid of him," said a coworker who seemed to care a lot more than I did about the situation.

I was twenty-five years old when the President who played saxophone on late-night television, appeared on MTV and weighed the pros and cons of boxers vs. briefs, was under fire for alleged sexual misconduct, including having an affair with White House intern, Monica Lewinsky (who once asked me for a piece of gum on a flight to JFK many years later).

Is this how the century was going to end? We were on the cusp of the year 2000 and all we cared about were blowjobs and boxers. What a massive fall from grace we had from the beginning of the decade when kids like me had the world at their fingertips because our music and culture said we did. Yeah, we were rough around the edges and could stand to turn the positivity on our personalities up a little bit, but we had a voice. Dare I say we even had some hope.

The '90s were one of those decades that felt like a lifetime. The personal and societal ups and downs were more than I was capable of shouldering, and it felt like it was only going to get heavier. I didn't know what was to come but whatever it was, I was almost convinced I didn't want to find out.

We entered the decade with a bang and ended it with a blowjob. Nothing had changed and yet everything changed. They say numbers don't lie. We know this isn't always completely accurate as people can sometimes play with numbers a bit to fit whichever narrative they're trying to push at any given moment. In 1999 however, as with all the years that came before it since album sales were tracked by Billboard, (Billboard began its practice of tracking record sales in 1945 with many variations and chart types added since then) Billboard's chart numbers tell a very accurate story proving that the grunge and alternative era that dominated the musical and cultural world, was officially over.

Looking at the weekly breakdown as configured by Billboard, tracking the best-selling album per week for the entire year, it's not difficult to see that the music-listening and buying public had moved on from the music of the early and mid-'90s and had reverted to easier listening pop and copycat grunge and alternative. There were a couple of holdovers from the heyday of grunge, alternative, and hip-hop (along with a couple of newcomers who would become massively important going forward) sprinkled throughout the list, but it was obvious what the public wanted to listen to had changed. All the information here comes from Billboard's lists and findings and I'm including it to put into perspective how stark a change there was in what people at the very end of one of the most creative, diverse, and influential decades had decided to move on to.

Looking at who was on top of the weekly charts in 1999, it's like a who's who of pop, country, and "grunge lite" artists. Let me clarify one thing here.

CHAPTER 12 - 1999: BUBBLEGUM IS BACK

I'll be honest, I wasn't then, nor am I now, a fan of most of the rock music coming out in the late '90s. Some would call me a snob and that's fine, I understand it. It's more than that though. I lived through the birth, marriage, honeymoon, troubled times, and downfall of a genre that felt like it was created for me. The music I was seemingly groomed to fall in love with by the genres that influenced those making it like metal, punk, hardcore, and what some would call college music when I was a kid, had died right in front of my eyes.

When you're in your late teens through your mid-20s, the world can become a lonely and scary place. We all have our stories, and they vary in the degree of pain and seriousness. All we can deal with however is what our reality is and that becomes our world. I've had a rough go of just about everything in life, for various reasons and incidents, which I believe to be responsible for my lifelong struggle with anxiety and depression, countless hours in therapy, and my dark and sometimes fatalistic view of the world. I don't care who you are, when things are heavy and you find solace in something to make everything lighter, even for just a fleeting moment in time, you hang onto it for dear life. I could've turned to drugs, alcohol, gambling, or any other destructive vice that numbed the pain.

Luckily it was music that provided the high of escapism, giving me the ability to dream about a time when my life could be intertwined with the one thing I was made for. Perhaps now is that time, we shall see. What is my point in writing all of this? It's my long-winded way of understanding how the music I discuss in this book and the culture and generation it spawned have meant more to me and my well-being than just about anything else I've ever encountered in life. Am I a music snob? Probably. Am I indebted to the unlikely and ultimately far-reaching music scene hatched from a city just under 2,900 miles away from where I grew up, absolutely. Back to the charts.

Names like Garth Brooks, Britney Spears, Backstreet Boys, TLC, Dixie Chicks, Celine Dion, and Santana occupied the charts for the longest amount of time in 1999. The Backstreet Boys spent the most time in the number one weekly spot covering 10 non-consecutive weeks. This was it folks, pop music once again ruled the world. It wasn't that long ago that Nirvana had supplanted the King of Pop at the top of the charts, marking the official takeover of grunge and alternative music. It was fun while it lasted because seven years after Nirvana's dominance, it was all over. A boy band out of Orlando, Florida that didn't write its music (Max Martin was the songwriter for most of the hits and has written or co-written songs for Britney Spears, Pink, Usher, Taylor Swift, Katy Perry, Bon Jovi, and dozens of others) had somehow changed the global radio station from "Smells Like Teen Spirit" to "I Want it That Way" and no one seemed to blink an eye.

With the advantage of time and hindsight, things can sometimes tend to go unnoticed or overlooked when discussing history. Music and pop culture are not immune to this practice. As stated earlier, the darkness and heaviness of the grunge sound from the early '90s had struck a chord with kids of a certain age, living in a specific culture, who'd just about had enough of their lives and rode the wave of music that healed them. Things can only last for so long.

As we grew older and started to graduate college, move out of our parent's houses, and start careers, we took the music with us as if it were luggage. We didn't leave it behind for the younger kids right behind us to absorb. As Bob Dylan so famously once sang, "The times, they are a-changin,'" and change they did. The pop world was tired of darkness, depression, and suicide, and like during the '80s, wanted its music to be lighthearted and fun. All fluff, with zero substance. People needed a break and MTV and Top 40 radio gave it to them.

Backstreet Boys' preeminence was massive. *Millennium* sold 1,134,000 copies in its first week of release, breaking the previous record held by Garth Brooks for single-week record sales. *Millennium* sold nearly 500,000 copies in the U.S. on its first day alone, and became the best-selling album of 1999,

CHAPTER 12 - 1999: BUBBLEGUM IS BACK

selling 9,445,732 albums in all. It remained on the Billboard chart for 93 weeks, eventually selling over 13 million copies in the United States.

I mentioned the "sprinkles" a little earlier about some rock artists that you'd expect a Billboard chart from the '90s to include and they were Rage Against the Machine, Nine Inch Nails, and Korn. Hip-hop was still incredibly strong and made a great showing on the best-selling albums list as well with records by DMX, Foxy Brown, Nas, Eve, and The Notorious B.I.G.

ok, so maybe all was not lost when it comes to rock and rap from the early and middle part of the decade, there were some significant heavyweights still representing. What I haven't mentioned from this list yet however were the bands that "replaced" grunge in the commercial and public eye, and that's really where the scene was dealt its death knell. Creed and Limp Bizkit spent a combined six weeks occupying the number one weekly spot with their albums *Human Clay* and *Significant Other* respectively. Although I saw the scene from the early and mid-'90s dying right before my eyes around this time, I still held so much regard for those times. Most of what was happening in 1999 and the year or so before, didn't feel the same to me as those earlier years had. I wasn't connected to most of the new bands. It no longer felt genuine to me.

I remember a great story Tracy Bonham told me about her experience at Woodstock 99 and it sums up how she and I felt about the new scene. "There was this moment I shared with Cheryl Crow at Woodstock 99. I had just gotten off a helicopter because they were flying me in, which was the weirdest thing ever, and DMX was on the stage. We noticed all these white, aggressive men, jumping, screaming, and fighting in the crowd, and Cheryl and I looked at each other and said, "This is fucked!"

Describing what it was like when Nirvana burst onto the scene in 1991 to someone who wasn't there will never come close to witnessing the phenomenon yourself. That's true in all walks of life. Sometimes you must see it to believe it. As with *Nevermind* in 1991, *The Slim Shady LP*, the second studio album by Detroit rapper Eminem, changed the future of music and launched the career of one of the most influential and commercially successful musicians of all time. The '90s opened with a game changer and closed with one. Different genres and mostly different fan bases aside, *Nevermind* and *The Slim Shady LP* would largely define and secure the 1990s as one of the most important and revered decades in music history.

Released by Aftermath Entertainment and Interscope Records, *The Slim Shady LP* was a gigantic exclamation point on a decade of music that had defied the odds and would go on to influence music of all genres for the next 30 years. By the time this record was released, Eminem had made very small waves within the music industry. He had two previous releases, his debut album *Infinite* in 1996 and the EP, *The Slim Shady EP* released at the end of 1997 to little fanfare. The EP did catch the ears and eyes of Jimmy Iovine (co-founder of Interscope Records) and former N.W.A. superstar, Dr. Dre. however, and as they say in the business, the rest is history. Slim Shady was a character created by Eminem (real name Marshall Bruce Mathers III) designed as the rapper's alter-ego. With lyrical themes of violence, drugs, poverty, and horror, and a production style mix of West Coast hip-hop and G-funk, the combination struck a chord with lost and angry youth the world over. Not unlike Nirvana before him, Eminem found common ground with a fan base dying for what he had to offer.

With *The Slim Shady LP* being released at the beginning of 1999, it gave the world almost a full year to witness and absorb Eminem's rise to power in both the musical and cultural landscapes. The album sold 283,000 copies in its first week and debuted at number two behind TLC's *FanMail* on Billboard's Top 200 Album chart. The record remained on the *Billboard* 200 for 100 weeks. It also reached number one on the R&B/hip-hop Albums chart, staying on that chart for 92 weeks. On November 15, 2000, the album was certified quadruple platinum by the RIAA.

CHAPTER 12 – 1999: BUBBLEGUM IS BACK

Something that was uniquely a part of the '90s music culture was its inclusivity and openness to new music. When hip-hop started, it was mainly an African American art form. Much like Blues and Motown before it, most of its creators were black, but the music would always cross over to include a white audience. This is not a book on the record industry's exploitation of black artists throughout the history of music, but just know that racial lines had always been drawn by the corporate tastemakers of the day. Unfortunately, race plays a large role in just about everything we do as human beings, and music certainly has not been able to escape this ignorant trend.

The '90s music scene did make some serious inroads when it came to people of all races, religions, and genders being accepted as top-flight artists with influence and staying power. Eminem, being a white man in a genre dominated by black artists, was a talking point at the time. The acceptance of rap music's pioneers and contemporaries of Eminem, along with his lyrical prowess and overall musical skill, helped allow him to sit on top of the genre's world for a long time and since becoming recognized as one of the greatest hip-hop artists of all time. In an article by Lynette Holloway entitled, "The Angry Appeal of Eminem is Cutting Across Racial Lines" published in The New York Times in 2002, Stephen Hill, the then Vice President of BET (Black Entertainment Television) had this to say about Eminem's musical and cultural significance:

"Eminem gets a pass in the same vein that back during segregation black folks had to be better than average, had to be the best, to be accepted . . . he is better than the best. In his own way, he is the best lyricist, alliterator, and enunciator out there in hip-hop music. In terms of rapping about the pain that other disenfranchised people feel, there is no one better at their game than Eminem."

Many rappers have praised Eminem as well. Legendary artist Rakim of Eric B. and Rakim fame once said, "Eminem is tough, man. I don't care what color he is. I don't care about none of that. Real artists respect real artists, man . . .

I tell people to this day. If Em was black, he'd be the next Muhammad Ali, man."

Eminem sparked a renewed love for hip-hop in 1999 and the world took notice. According to Nielsen SoundScan, he was the best-selling artist from 2000-2009 in the United States and would eventually become one of the best-selling artists of all time with more than 220 million records sold worldwide. The history of modern music cannot be discussed without Eminem in it, and it all started in the 1990s.

Throughout the '90s but getting more prominent as the decade was ending, electronic music was making waves and grabbing kids' attention, further proving that grunge was dead and buried as a cultural player. EDM, techno, ambient, trip-hop, house, electronica, trance, and DJ culture were the new flavors of the day, and all those genres and sub-genres couldn't be further away from the early '90s Seattle scene that once dominated the world. Artists like Moby, Sasha and John Digweed, Ferry Corsten, Paul Oakenfold, and others became global sensations. Even Madonna jumped on the bandwagon releasing her album, *Ray of Light*.

Discussing this trend with Kristina Marie whom I spoke with earlier and who has roots in trance music looking back on its ascension during the 1990s. "Becoming involved in dance music definitely stems from those early, transformative days at MTV because it was my first real job. It sticks with you. It's why I'm so interested to think about the people who pivoted and embraced dance music back then. Some of them did very badly and some did quite well. I think U2 was a disaster when they tried to do dance music. Even David Bowie did a dance album, and it was a spectacular fail." As our conversation continued though we shared our feelings on how that's not necessarily a bad thing. Evolving as an artist should never be shunned. Artists should challenge not just the status quo, but their audience as well. Marie put it well saying, "Sometimes people just eat what's served. It takes a little bit of

CHAPTER 12 - 1999: BUBBLEGUM IS BACK

insight, time, and focus to figure out what makes good music, good music. Sometimes people need a shift in their thinking to pivot."

Along with the obvious change on radio, MTV, and the album charts, something else happened in 1999 that would deal a crucial blow, not just to the grunge and alternative movement, but to the entire way the world would consume music forever. On June 1, 1999, a company would launch, crippling the music industry as we knew it and sending artists, fans, and record companies alike into a frenzy that we still haven't fully escaped from today. The company was Napster.

Napster was a peer-to-peer file-sharing application primarily associated with digital audio file distribution. Founded by Shawn Fanning and Sean Parker, Napster was about to change the music industry forever. Audio shared on the service was typically encoded in the MP3 format making it easily shareable and accessible. As the software became popular, the company encountered legal battles over copyright infringement and closed its doors in 2001. Napster filed for bankruptcy in June 2002.

The peer-to-peer model utilized by Napster involved a centralized database that indexed a complete list of all songs being shared from connected clients. While effective, the service could not function without the central database, which was hosted by Napster and eventually forced to shut down.

Napster's assets were acquired by Roxio, and it re-emerged as an online music store known as Napster. Tech giant Best Buy later purchased the service and merged it with its Rhapsody streaming service on December 1, 2011. In 2016, Napster's original branding returned when Rhapsody was renamed Napster.

As you might imagine, a firestorm of controversy was underway once word got out as to how easy it was to share files containing recorded music *for free*! Again, this was 1999, not 2019 or even 2009. Obtaining music for free, using links or a click of a button was virtually unheard of back then and to the artists and the record industry, this new technology was akin to Armageddon. To that point, one of the biggest and richest bands on the planet was the first to publicly battle Napster in what they saw as a fight between right and wrong, good and evil.

It would be difficult to argue that heavy metal band Metallica wasn't one of the biggest bands on the planet in 1999 and had just as much power within the music industry as anyone else at the time. When people with that sort of influence take a loud and aggressive stance against something, the world pays attention. The band's drummer and co-founder, Lars Ulrich became the poster boy for the music industry against Fanning and Parker's free music machine. Incensed by what the band argued was "copyright infringement, racketeering, and unlawful use of digital audio interface devices," Metallica et al. v. Napster, Inc. became the first case of an artist suing the peer-to-peer file-sharing company. Metallica was suing for a minimum of $10 million in damages at a rate of $100,000 per illegally downloaded song.

The band produced a list of 335,435 Napster users who were allegedly sharing the band's songs online in violation of copyright laws. Metallica demanded that their songs be banned from file sharing and that the users responsible for sharing their music be banned from the service. This led to over 300,000 users being banned from Napster. The lawsuit also named several universities to be held accountable for allowing students to illegally download music on their networks. To put it lightly, things got ugly.

In March 2001, the federal district court ruling over the case issued a preliminary injunction in Metallica's favor pending the case's resolution. The injunction ordered Napster to place a filter on the program within 72 hours or be shut down. Napster was forced to remove all copyrighted songs by Metallica.

Other artists including Dr. Dre, several record companies, and the RIAA (Recording Industry Association of America) subsequently filed their lawsuits which led to the termination of an additional 230,142 Napster accounts. On July 12, 2001, Napster settled with Metallica and Dr. Dre after Bertelsmann AG BMG became interested in purchasing the rights to Napster for $94

CHAPTER 12 - 1999: BUBBLEGUM IS BACK

million. The deal fell through, and Napster was forced to file for bankruptcy and liquidate its assets. All of this was because nineteen-year-old Shawn Fanning and his friends around the country wanted to trade music in the MP3 format. Fanning wanted to increase the number of files available and involve more people by creating a way for users to browse each other's files and talk to each other.

Upon Napster's launch, the number of registered users doubled every 5–6 weeks. In February 2001, Napster had roughly 80 million monthly users. To put that into perspective regarding its popularity, the mainstream website Yahoo had 54 million monthly users at that time. At its peak, Napster facilitated nearly 2 billion file transfers per month and had an estimated net worth of between $60 and 80 million dollars.

Fanning designed Napster as a searching and indexing program, meaning that the files were not downloaded from Napster's servers but rather from a peer's computer. Users had to download another program, allowing them to interact with Napster's servers. When users log onto their Napster account, MusicShare, the other downloaded program, would read the names of the MP3 files that the user had made public and would then communicate with Napster's servers so a complete list of all public files from all users could be obtained.

Once logged into Napster a user would simply enter the name of the file they wanted to download and hit the search button to view a list of all the sources that contained the file. The user would click the download button, and the Napster server would communicate with the host's MusicShare browser to facilitate a connection and begin the download. Essentially Napster was started for broke college kids to enjoy music and talk to one another. Instead, it destroyed a decades-long way of doing business within the record industry and triggered a new way of communicating, sharing, and delivering music for free. If this sounds familiar, it should. In essence, Napster was the birth of streaming music which would ultimately go on to change the consumption of music forever.

The more things change, the more they stay the same. Music and culture had already moved on from what was for me and millions of my closest friends, the glory days of the early '90s, but living in a crazy and violent world as a 26-year-old still looking for answers remained eerily the same as when I was 18 in 1991. Be it civil unrest in the inner cities, the unfortunate predictability of continued school shootings in America highlighted by the infamous Columbine shooting in April of '99 where 13 people lost their lives, or the news of nearly 10,000 people being killed because of a cyclone in India, we were all still staring at a bleak and unwritten future. The music I had been turning to for quite some time now still existed but was no longer leading the cultural charge for my generation. We had been put out to pasture by 1999, and it didn't sit all that well with me.

I contemplated sending that letter I mentioned earlier in the book to my parents but held off for a few more years. I wanted to fix what was wrong by myself, embarrassed by the thoughts and potential actions written by my hand inside that letter. I finally hit rock bottom in the early 2000s, living alone with no job and no money. It was time to either do what the letter asserted or send it to my parents hoping there was a better outcome to find. Wanting to live, I thankfully sent that letter, had a mini-intervention, went back to therapy, and have lasted long enough to get married, have two amazing children, and write this book.

Most people in my life have never heard of the letter or the story behind it until the publication of *SLACKER*. I'm sure it's easy to understand why. I mean, it took me several years from the time I wrote the words, "I no longer see the purpose in living" until I finally sent it to my parents. It's also taken me several years to write this book and include that story in it. For some, the phrase "music saved my life" may be a cliche, but for me, it's a fact. I hope that

CHAPTER 12 - 1999: BUBBLEGUM IS BACK

you find this music or whichever genre you love to be as important to you as the early '90s grunge and alternative movement was for me. More importantly, though, I hope telling my story of feeling lost, looking for answers, and losing purpose but clinging onto something like music to pull me through, (along with asking for help from loved ones and professionals), gives you the hope and confidence it takes to pull through as well if you ever find yourself in a similar situation. There's a lot of great music to listen to and learn about, make sure you're here for it all.

CHAPTER 13
FROM A SLACKER: MORE OF A CONFESSION THAN A CHAPTER

Hi, my name is Rob and I'm a SLACKER.

A card-carrying member of Generation X with the musical DNA to prove it. I'm a product of divorce, single-parent upbringing, therapy, and MTV.

I'm a latchkey kid who was left alone to figure it all out for myself, but never quite did. I'm still full of questions and teen spirit angst with more targets for my slings and arrows now, but the problem is, no one bleeds from the puncture wounds anymore.

I'm a remnant of the forgotten generation as the spoiled meat between the doughy sides of baby boomer and millennial bread. I rot in the middle as they argue over who has the bigger slice.

I've been looking California and feeling Minnesota for over three decades now (if you know, you know), but I'm still alive . . . we're all still alive, and I'd have it no other way.

A reluctant icon once sang, "Teenage angst has paid off well, now I'm bored and old," almost prophesying how this unlikely magic carpet ride would end.

I've referenced it before, but that is the first line, from the first song, off In Utero by Nirvana, the follow-up to the biggest album of the era, Nevermind.

Kurt wasn't shy about his feelings regarding his newly anointed sainthood, but we didn't care, we only wanted more.

Kurt never did grow old though, he left that to the rest of us.

Now that we're more than 30 years on from the start of the most improbable success story that was the early '90s grunge and alternative movement, we should relish in the fact that we were there for it all, have the music to wash over us, get to introduce it to our children, and somehow morph into the best version of a slacker that anyone could've ever imagined.

ACKNOWLEDGMENTS

I DON'T KNOW THE EXACT AGE WHEN I BEGAN READING WITH ANY SEMBLANCE OF COMPREHENsion, but whatever age it was, I remember reading about music. *Cream*, *Hit Parader*, *Rolling Stone*, and a little later, *Spin* magazines were all I wanted to consume. I read every feature, interview, and review. Any book I could find in a store or library that had anything to do with my favorite artists, I had to have. Along with documentaries about music and MTV, my quest for musical knowledge continued. That was my foundation, my education. Beginning in the late '70s through this very moment that you're reading these words, the writers, authors, and filmmakers who created that content were my teachers. If it weren't for them, *SLACKER* could never have happened. Thank you all!

In 2015, with one young child at home and another on the way, I was surprisingly and unceremoniously laid off from my job in corporate America. I wasn't the only one that they canned, there were about twenty or so very good, hard-working people who were laid off. Ya know, it was time to outsource our jobs because we got just a little too good at what we did, and I guess the board members all needed an extra vacation home or two so away we went. I'm telling you this so you can understand the mental and emotional place this put me and my wife in at that time. To put it mildly, it was rough. Probably not the best time to tell my wife that I was going to write full-time and start an independent record label. Now, I eventually got another job and then another one after that and hated them both. I worked on my writing and label while I was working these jobs. Something had to give. I was at my breaking point. I needed to do something I loved for my sanity and to one day show my children that you shouldn't do anything you hate because it can cripple your soul. You need to find happiness in what you do. It's not that my wife didn't agree with this philosophy, but being the pragmatic one in the marriage when it comes to fiscal decisions, saying she was nervous is a massive understatement. To her credit though, she knew I needed to follow my heart and do what I loved, knowing that it would likely come with no pay at first and probably cost us money. That's exactly what happened. She believed in me though and while she's always been an incredibly hard worker and extremely successful in her career, she did even more to try and make it easier for all of us. I would have never started my record label or have written the book you're reading right now if it weren't for her sacrifice and belief. Thank you, Amy, for making this dream of mine a reality. I love you!

From the instant I became a father, first to a daughter, and two and a half years later a son, I somehow knew that my life wasn't my own anymore. The decisions I'd make, the things I'd learn, and the way I would act in this world would all affect those two beautiful children in one way or another. It was my job to affect them in the most positive ways I could. Included in this thought process, it was always important for me to show them that life should be filled with as much happiness and joy as possible. I wanted them to understand that being passionate about something is a good thing and that if you love that thing enough, figure out a way to make a career out of it. It's ok to buck convention occasionally if you're good to other people and are genuinely happy with yourself. Peyton and Michael, you will never truly know how proud you make me or understand just how much I love you both. I'm inspired by

ACKNOWLEDGMENTS

the two of you every single day. Thank you both for being the awesome kids that you are and for being so supportive and excited throughout the entirety of the writing of this book. Daddy loves you so, so much!

I was probably around fourteen years old when I wrote my first poem. I'd always loved the idea of putting my thoughts down on paper in a way that was different than speaking those thoughts in a conversation. I felt like I had more to say while writing than talking. This feeling has never left me and the fact that I'm writing this in my very first book is proof of that. Just because I love to write, however, does not mean that I had any business writing a book. Published articles, reviews, interviews, and the like (as well as poetry) aside, the thought of writing a book was something, in my mind at least, that other people did. I read books; I don't write them. Until now. How did this happen? The better question is, who made this happen? I met Jenn Tuma-Young, Founder and CEO of Inspired Girl Enterprises and Publisher at Inspired Girl Publishing Group (Inspired By You Books is one of their imprints which my book is published under) through fellow author, Denise Cesare. I knew Denise had written a book called *Moments in Motion with Love*, published by Inspired Girl, but knew nothing about the process. Denise and I met for coffee one day and I told her that I too was writing a book. I was about 30,000 words into it and had no idea where to go from there. After a few minutes of me describing the concept of the book, she immediately said that I needed to speak with Jenn, her publisher. I had nothing to lose since I had failed on all my attempts up until that point to get a publisher to get back to me about possible representation or collaboration. Denise emailed Jenn to make an introduction and about a month later (Jenn is quite the busy woman), we finally spoke. It was one of those conversations that should've been ten minutes but was probably forty. We clicked. I knew then that this idea of mine was going to come to life. With Jenn's expert guidance, knowledge, and ability to immerse herself in every call, meeting, zoom, email, and text that we shared over these last couple of years, *SLACKER* came to be. Jenn, you're AMAZ-

ING! As I'm fond of saying, no one does anything by themselves. This is true in the case of Inspired Girl Enterprises as well. Jenn surrounds herself with amazing talent and it shows in every corner of the company. I am grateful to all of the editors, designers, and creatives who worked on my book, as well as the advisors and leadership team at Inspired Girl. Jessica, Michael, Tony, Janelle, Andy, Roseanna worked especially hard to make sure my experience, my book, and the events surrounding it were a success! Thank you all (and everyone else behind the scenes) so much!

I referenced this idea earlier when I said that I'm fond of saying that no one does anything alone. I wholeheartedly believe in that philosophy, and I tend to quote one of my favorite musicians of all time when discussing the concept:

> *"And so now I'd like to say - people can change anything they want to. And that means everything in the world…Without people you're nothing."*
> – Joe Strummer of The Clash

Without the following people (listed alphabetically), who generously gave their time, passion, insights, and expertise to SLACKER, I'm not sure that I'd have a book to write. Each one of them enhanced the book beyond my wildest dreams, created a wonderful writing experience for me, and forged new friendships. I am fortunate to have you all with me along for this wild ride!

Thank you – Tracy Bonham, for your music, words, light, and strength. You're an inspiration! Chris Celona (Grunge Bible), your passion for music and life is something I wish everyone had so keep spreading the word by giving people a place to go and feel like they belong. Configa, we may have been born at different times in different countries but every time we spoke, I felt like I was talking with someone I'd known my entire life. Music can bring anyone together. Laura DeMartini, you are the perfect example of being so inspired by music that you make your life's work about helping others because of that inspiration and love. You are selfless beyond words, and I appreciate you very

ACKNOWLEDGMENTS

much. Dr. Donna Gaines, what can I say other than "you're a total badass"! Your knowledge, skill, and way with words were an absolute education for me. I can listen to you talk about music and culture all day. Nico Hoon, simply put, you're amazing. We've gotten to know one another a bit over the years and from our very first conversation to our most recent, you never cease to impress me. Thank you for sharing your thoughts on music and of course your dad (who I hold in tremendous regard) with me. It means more than you know. Dr. Kelly Jakubowski, the work you and your team have done and continue to do to help people through music is nothing short of astounding. We all thank you for it!! Don Jamieson, being a fan of your comedy and as co-host of That Metal Show for years, it was a pleasure getting to know you and discuss music with you. Your insights and perspectives were crucial to the story I was trying to tell, and you delivered my man, thank you! Kristina Marie, your passion for music and bringing people together in its name is needed and quite infectious. Thank you for sharing your stories and insights! Eileen Mercolino, talk about a "wow" factor, your stories of those early days with Mother Love Bone and Pearl Jam had me hanging on your every word. That, coupled with all the amazing accomplishments you've had over the course of your music and marketing career, (and still kicking ass today) really helped shape this book and I simply cannot thank you enough. Jared Miller, I'm positive you and I were in the same bars, venues, and shows throughout NYC in the early and mid-90s. I was a fan, and you were promoting and managing the bands I was there to see. Not only did your experiences help fill the book with great stories, but your photographs also make the book something bigger than just words. Thank you! John Richards, our conversation was so vital to *SLACKER* and to me personally. You embody everything I tried to say in the book about vulnerability and understanding and dealing with the mental health side of music from the late 80s through the mid-90s. I was able to be as open with my struggles throughout the book partially because you were so open with me. Jo-Ann Rogan, not only are you one of the truest examples of the DIY punk movement but you're also a kind and genuine person. Thank you for contributing to *SLACKER*. Speech, watching you perform with your band, Arrested Development at Lollapalooza '93, was a transformative musical moment for me. Already a big fan of hip-hop by then, AD's inclusion at Lollapalooza brought the rock and rap worlds together for me in a way that hadn't happened before. I've been listening and learning ever since. Vaden Todd Lewis, whenever a conversation about 90s music comes up, Toadies are one of the first bands I enter those conversations with. Your music and lyric writing struck a chord that's hard to duplicate. Getting to speak with you was an absolute pleasure, thank you! Joseph J. Williams, knowing that *SLACKER* was going to be largely based on the feelings and emotions conjured up by music that often discussed topics such as depression, suicide, and other mental health issues, I needed the expertise of a professional. Not only did I get that in you, but I also got an extremely knowledgeable music fan whose opinions and perspectives I respect deeply. Thank you for the advice and conversations.

Writing a book takes patience, encouragement, mentorship, coffee, silence, friendships, inspiration, people who can help you do things you can't, and sometimes the need to throw things around the room. In no particular order, the following people have helped with some or all of these things along the way. Warning, I may need you all again soon so get ready! A heartfelt thanks to: Kevin, Ingrid, and the entire staff at Main Street Coffee in Staten Island, NY where much of the book was researched and written, all my friends at the Great Kills Swim Club, my wonderful friends at IS 34 and PS 42, Mike Pellegrino, Noah Levy, Kevin Alexander, Keith R. Higgons, Jeff Murphy, Ed Lavezzo, Nicole Trainor, Lou Pellegrino, Adam Silvestri, Hayley Richman, and Morey Richman. You have all played significant roles in my life, and by association, this book, and just know that I love and value all of you.

A fair amount of this book discusses my childhood from several aspects.

ACKNOWLEDGMENTS

Some are good, some not so good. I tend to think most of us have our ups and downs from when we were kids and often, we carry them with us for the rest of our lives. As mentioned throughout *SLACKER*, I have forever scars that helped shape the person I became and continue to become. There were dark times that I wasn't sure I'd walk out of. I did, however, and music wasn't the only thing that got me through it all. I was lucky enough to grow up in a neighborhood that had dozens of families with kids my age. I'm friends with many of them to this very day and they all know who they are. Whether they were from the E 64th St. crew, grammar school, or high school, they all have my love!

There is one group though that has been with me since the ridiculously young age of six years old that without whom, I sometimes wonder where or who I'd be. Joe, Pobs, Shawn, and Sluggo (relax fellas, I listed you alphabetically by first initial), my brothers from other mothers, it's been forty-five years and counting. Let's shoot for another forty-five together. Love you guys!

It's safe to say that my first exposure to music came from a couple of small AM radios in my mom's house when I was growing up. Hearing the likes of Elvis, Chuck Berry, The Beatles, Stones, singer/songwriters of the '70s, and the music of Motown as a kid planted the seeds that grew into a full-blown love and need of music. My mom was also the one who recognized that something was off with me around the time I was nine years old and immediately acted. I love you and I am forever grateful. Growing up in a single-parent home from the age of five was difficult, but my mother always did her best to shield us from the many difficulties and disappointments surrounding us. Looking back now I can see that my mother, Diane Janicke, led the most selfless life any human being could, all for the benefit of me and my younger sister. Thank you, Mom, no one has rooted harder for me in life than you have. I may not say it often, but it is a fact I've known and will know for the rest of my life.

My first (and still to this day) best friend, my sister Janine, has always been there for me. We are close in years, only a year and eleven months apart, but even closer in connection. Her family, my brother-in-law Paul, niece Gabriella, and nephew Paulie have been a tremendous part of my life, and I love you all!

It's a well-known fact that when you get married you not only gain a spouse, but you also gain an entire family. I could not have asked for a better group of people to now call family than my in-laws Eilean and Paul Kosinski, brother-in-law Paul and his family, Pam, PJ, Lily, and Alex, and brother-in-law David and his family, Erica, Tyler, Jaxson, and Eric. And a special tribute (and RIP) to Grams and Gramps. I want to thank you all for accepting me into the beautiful family you've all had a hand in building. Love you all!

To ALL my friends and family. I'm beyond lucky to say there are too many to mention in the space I have, THANK YOU for supporting and believing in me. Even if we don't speak or see one another regularly, please know that I think of you often and fondly. In a world that can easily make you feel alone at times, I know, because of all of you, that I will never, ever be alone.

To my cousin and inspirational powerhouse Angel…you left us WAY too soon. There isn't a day that goes by where I'm not thinking of our life chats over coffee or brainstorming ideas for our record label. We even had plans to write a book together and now, in a way, we did. Thank you for guiding me and instilling the confidence that I needed to follow my dreams the way you followed yours. I love and miss you. Angel D'Apice (5/16/66 – 8/5/21)

SLACKER – 1991, Teen Spirit Angst, and the Generation It Created was written for music lovers by a music lover. I'm a rabid fan of music, particularly the music discussed within these pages, just like I'm assuming you are. We are the same. In my eyes, we are all slackers in the very best way possible. I never pass up an opportunity to have a conversation about music, its impact on society, culture, or who we are as human beings. It's my favorite topic to think about and talk about. I cherish those conversations. And now, because these words have been recorded in book form, I feel like I can have a conver-

ACKNOWLEDGMENTS

sation with anyone who reads the book, anywhere, at any time. That is a privilege you have all afforded me and I cannot express properly how that makes me feel. Without you, the readers, *SLACKER* would just be a long message to myself. While I guess that's ok, how incredibly amazing is it though that I get to share the message with all of you? You have all literally made my dreams come true. Thank you!

www.ingramcontent.com/pod-product-compliance
Lightning Source LLC
Chambersburg PA
CBHW030107170426
43198CB00009B/522